Forex 2021: The Best Methods For Forex Trading.

Make Money Trading Online With The $11,000

per Month Guide

David Uchiha

TABLE OF CONTENTS

INTRODUCTION

Welcome to the beginning of this journey. In this book, we are going to explore the FOREX market and what it represents for investors all over the world. This book has been written with the novice investor in mind. As such, we will be covering the basics of FOREX, how you can get into the market, and how you can make the most out of your investments. Best of all, we will be presenting all of this in an easy to digest format. Sure, we are going to be covering some rather technical terminology. Nevertheless, we'll make sure that you get the information you need in a way that resonates with you.

This book is for all of those folks who are looking to get into the FOREX market but don't really know how to go about it. This is why each chapter focuses specifically on an aspect related to currency markets and how you can benefit from placing your money in FOREX. The main thing to keep in mind is that you can make sustainable gains by following the guidelines that we present. In this manner, you can be sure that you won't lose out on the deals you make.

In addition, please bear in mind that investing in financial markets always poses a risk. After all, there are no sure deals. Every time you enter a trade, you can expect to carry some degree of risk. This is important to note as you can't always expect to make massive profits. In fact, highly successful FOREX investors make money by multiplying minor deals over and over again. When you are able to do this, you will find that making a consistent return on your deals is far easier than you might have thought.

So, what are you waiting for?

Let's begin on the journey that will lead you from the couch to FOREX investment success. While it does take some time and effort to master the overall scheme of the FOREX market, you will find that this guide will provide you with all of the essentials you need to hit the ground running. You won't have to scour the internet to find a credible source of information. Everything you need is right here.

Please bear in mind that making money in FOREX is based on the time and effort you are willing to put into the research needed to place successful deals. The good news is that this guide will provide you with the guidelines you need to make successful trades. While you may not win every single time, you can rest assured that you will come out on top, most of the time.

That's where the real money is made.

One last thing: we ask that you read through this guide to the end before placing your first trades. It's essential that you gain an understanding of the entire scope of FOREX trading prior to getting started. That way, you can be sure that you won't make any initial mistakes that could cost you lots of money.

Let's get on with it!

CHAPTER 1

Introduction To Forex Trading

FOREX is a financial market that deals in currency trading exclusively. Now, please don't be confused with other financial markets, such as the stock market. Stocks are completely different types of financial investments that don't have a direct relation with FOREX. This is why we will spend the length of this book discussing currencies.

It's important to keep in mind that currency refers to the type of money that every country issues. This is the underlying fundamental tenet of FOREX. We are talking about comparing the valuation of each country's currency as it relates to another. As such, you need to understand that money and currency are two different things.

In general, money can be any commodity known to man. Historically, several commodities have served as money, such as salt, feathers, cocoa beans, and cattle. However, gold and silver became the main commodities that have served as money throughout history.

The reason why gold and silver are not currency any longer is due to the fact that they are in short supply. It can be tough and expensive to mine gold and silver out of the ground. Therefore, our modern economy needed to find another commodity that could serve as money while ensuring the growth of a modern economy.

This is where the modern currencies we know today come into play. Depending on the country you live in, you will be dealing with one currency or another. Also, depending on your lifestyle, you may be dealing with multiple currencies. In that case, you can appreciate the interaction that goes on among multiple currencies while also understanding the valuation that exists among different currencies.

As a result, buying and selling currencies is a natural occurrence in modern financial markets. Of course, you don't need to become a big-time investor to take part in this type of market. A very simple example of how you can participate in currency trading is when you travel. When you exchange your country's currency for that of the country you are visiting, you have placed a currency exchange trade. The main difference is that such transactions don't have speculative purposes.

This is an important thing to note here.

Speculation refers to the motivation behind making trades. When you place a trade for speculative purposes, you are doing so with the hope of making money on another trade later on. In other words, you are looking to buy low and sell high just as you would with stocks, bonds, or any other type of financial asset.

Throughout this book, we will be discussing currency pairs. In order for a FOREX trade to take place, you need to become familiar with the various types of currency pairs that are commonly traded. When you have pairs that are commonly traded, such as the Euro and the US Dollar, we call these "correlated pairs." These pairs usually have the highest trade volume and offer you the best opportunity to make money.

By the same token, you can place trades in "uncorrelated pairs," meaning that they don't have a direct relation to one another. In such cases, the trades are riskier but can offer a great deal of potential profits.

This is why it's important to fully understand the dynamics of the FOREX market so that you can make the best investment decisions based on your expectations and investment strategy.

Types of FOREX Markets

There are various types of FOREX markets you can choose to invest in. Depending on your expectations, experience, and interests, you can choose to invest in any of these markets. The best part of all is that you can dip your toes into all markets at the same time. However, we don't recommend this right away. It's always best to master one market before moving on to the next. Eventually, you'll be able to make money in various types of markets at the same time.

Also, please keep in mind that understand how each market works is both a question of practice and experience. So, it's always a good idea to study the dynamics of each market. That way, when you are set to market some money, you know what to expect. Moreover, you'll be ready for anything that might come your way.

The Spot Market

By far, this is the most common market within the FOREX domain. The reason why it's called "spot" it's because the transactions which take place in this market happen at the current exchange rate. Please bear in mind that exchange rates vary all the time. Therefore, you need to keep a close eye on where they are heading. Since exchange rates are determined by market forces, they can shift significantly in a short time period.

In FOREX, "exchange rates" refer to the relative value on one currency to another. This means that exchange rates express how much one currency is worth with regard to another. As such, you may find that exchange rates function as a price when conducting trades. Depending on the movement of exchange rates, you can make or lose money.

The majority of the action happens in the spot market. This means that the largest volume of trading happens among currency pairs as they are traded based on current exchange rates. The degree with which trading volume increases or decreases is called "volatility." Volatility refers to the changes in the volume of trading. If the volume of trading doesn't change much, then there is little volatility. However, if there are sudden changes, then this would be considered volatility.

Additionally, volatility refers to the fluctuations in exchange rates themselves. When there is a high degree of volatility, there are significant shifts in exchange rates. Often, these shifts are nothing more than pennies on the dollar. Still, when multiplied by thousands, or even millions of dollars, the pennies suddenly add up. Therefore, it's important for you to keep this in mind.

When you set out to trade on the FOREX market, you will find that your trading platform will display exchange rates as they are being calculated through the act of supply and demand. Supply refers to the amount of one currency available on the market, while demand refers to the number of buyers who wish to purchase it. When there is a balance among these two forces, exchange rates remain relatively stable. When there is a significant shift on one side or another, then exchange rates may suddenly swing up or down.

While violent swings in exchange rates are not unheard of, they are uncommon unless there are forces that compel investors to dump one currency and seek refuge in another. Consider this situation:

Investors are loading up on the currency of country X. This causes supply to be in short order as more and more investors are interested in taking positions in this currency. Then, country X announces they have been hit severely by falling oil prices, causing them to default on their external debt. This causes investors to panic and begin dumping their positions in this currency. Since investors are now looking to find shelter, they begin to dump currency X and buy US Dollars. This causes the relative price of the US Dollar to go up in relation to currency X.

This example might seem a bit extreme, but it has happened throughout history. So, it's not uncommon to see such situations, especially in countries that don't have a stable political situation. As we will discuss later on, it's important for investors to be cognizant of a country's political stability and economic outlook. These are the main factors that can help you determine if you are getting into a safe deal, or you might be opening up yourself to unwanted risk.

Futures Market

The futures market, as the name implies, deals with transactions that will be completed at some point in the future. The futures market is governed by contracts between buyer and seller. In these contracts, the seller agrees to sell at a specific exchange rate while the buyer agrees to purchase at that specific exchange rate.

These contracts are conducted for two main reasons:

The first reason, both buyer and seller are concerned about volatility. As such, they are keen on making sure that they can lock in a given exchange rate so they can avoid having to pay a higher rate or having to sell at a lower one. This is done for purely speculative reasons. Now, it should be noted that not all futures contracts create an obligation to either buyer or seller. In fact, some contracts are called "options." Under the concept of an option, investors can choose not to buy or sell under the specific terms of the contract itself. These provide a great deal of flexibility, especially when volatility is quite high.

The second reason is related to supply. There are times when investors foresee the possibility of shortages in the supply of a currency. So, they might take out a futures contract in order to ensure that they have a guaranteed supply of a specific currency. Later on, these contracts can be sold to other investors who are looking to ensure the supply of a given currency. In such cases, you would not be profiting from the sale of the currency itself. Rather, you would be profiting from the sale of the contract.

Lastly, the futures market is a very important part of FOREX, as it allows investors to protect their positions in the long run. This is a clear difference from the spot market, as the spot market mostly deals with short-term deals. In contrast, the futures market deals with trades that may be conducted months into the future. It all depends on the specific terms of the contract itself.

Forward Market

In the forward market, the transactions that occur are generally the same as the futures market, with the difference that the terms and conditions are customizable to suit the needs of the investors. As such, any number of conditions can be used to trigger the contract. The most common condition is time. The contract would have a specific expiration date in which the trade is executed one the deadline is reached. Also, contracts may include very specific conditions such as exchange rates, volatility, and even the number of trades placed. For instance, a forward contract may stipulate that if the two parties engage in five trades over a two-week period, then the forward contract is executed, thereby causing a sixth trade to happen.

This example highlights how conditions can be set up to meet any number of needs so long as the parties involved agree to them. This offers a great deal of flexibility that cannot be found in the spot market. So, do keep this in mind as you may find yourself in need to engage in custom deals, especially if you can find a willing trade partner.

Factors of Influence in the FOREX Market

The previous example highlights the fact that there are many factors that can influence FOREX markets. As such, it's important for you to do your research before jumping into any sort of trade. Most importantly, you need to be aware of the dangers and risks that come with investing in FOREX without understanding the underlying fundamentals supporting the deal you are making.

That is why we are going to look at technical analysis and fundamental analysis as it pertains to the FOREX market.

Technical Analysis

This is the most common research approach in FOREX. Technical analysis consists in the use of statistical tools and models to analyze the behavior patterns of individual currencies and currency pairs. With technical analysis, you can relatively predict the shifts in exchange rates, particularly if you have a great deal of information to work with. As such, you can construct models that will help you make decisions on what currency pairs to invest in and how you can determine how they will work out.

With technical analysis, you will need to read charts and graphs. These charts will reveal the type of information you need to digest in order to place deals. Such information includes trading volume, exchange rates, and trends.

Speaking of trends, recognizing trends is the single most important aspect of FOREX trading. When you learn to recognize trends, you can determine what a currency's valuation might be at any point in the future. Most importantly, you won't be guessing at what price shifts might occur. In fact, you may find yourself making reasonable assumptions based on the information you have analyzed.

When analyzing trends, you will encounter the term known as a "moving average." A moving average consists of the average exchange rate over a given period of time. For instance, you can calculate the moving average by determining the average exchange rate every hour over the course of two trading days. This will provide you with a glimpse of the currency's behavior.

By the same token, trend can help you determine if it is bullish or bearish. A bullish trend means that that one currency's value is gaining in relation to another. A bearish trend means that one currency's value is diminishing in relation to another.

On the whole, technical analysis is considered to be the cornerstone of FOREX investing. When you are able to harness the power that comes with this kind of information, you will be able to make sound investment decisions every single time.

Fundamental Analysis

The other core element of FOREX market analysis is called "fundamental analysis." Fundamental analysis takes into consideration political, economic, and social factors that might affect a currency's valuation. Please keep in mind that the valuation of a currency depends on a country's overall situation more than what investors perceive to be the value of a currency. In fact, investors will look to the relative stability of a country as an indicator of a currency's value.

This is why the US Dollar, the Euro, and the Swiss Franc are all considered to be "safe" currencies. On the other hand, when you have a country that does not have a stable political situation, you will find that investors will try to avoid putting too many assets into that currency as there is no guarantee where that currency's valuation will head.

Moreover, political factors can literally make, or break, a currency's valuation. Earlier, we highlighted how oil prices can tank a currency's value. Additionally, currency may be propped up by news of strong economic data. This implies that countries that receive positive reviews from economic forecasters may find their currency experiencing an increase in its value as investors will perceive it to be "safer" as opposed to other currencies which may lack greater backing from their country's government or economic outlook.

So, it's best to keep an eye on social, economic, and political news as being aware of these factors can keep your investments safe while avoiding serious losses.

Basic Trading Terms

In this section, we are going to discuss some basic terminology.

- **Cross rate**. This is the value of one currency expressed in another. Commonly, you will find a cross rate to be expressed in the following manner: CHFEUR. In this example, the Swiss Franc (CHF) is expressed in terms of the Euro (EUR). Therefore, when reading the cross rate, you get the value of the Swiss Franc expressed in Euros. So, a cross rate of 1.15 means that for every CHF, you get 1.15 EUR.

- **Exchange Rate**. Exchange rates serve to determine the relative price of one currency in terms of another. Now, you might think that cross rates and exchange rates are the same things. On the surface, they are. The difference lies in that cross rates just compare the value of one currency to another. In fact, you might find that currencies that don't have an exchange rate between them may be to peg their value to a third currency such as the US Dollar. In this case, exchange rates refer specifically to the valuation between two currencies without having to use a third one as a reference. For instance, the exchange rate for the USDEUR pairing may be 0.90. This means that you get 90 cents on the Euro for every US Dollar. Also, cross rates are not necessarily negotiable. However, exchange rates are subject to market forces and can shift at any time.

- **Leverage**. In essence, leverage means that you enter a trade that is greater than the actual amount of money you are investing in. For instance, if you have $100 for a trade, you enter a position that's $1,000. This is a 10 x 1 leverage. If you win, you collect your earnings on $1,000 and not $100. However, if you lose, then you will have to make up the difference of $1,000. In this scenario, you could end up completely wiped out. Novice investors are not cleared to trade using leverage. You need to build up your reputation, so to speak. Also, some trading platforms may ask you to deposit a sum of money as a guarantee that you can cover your margins should you fail to win a trade on leverage. If you trade on leverage and cannot cover the margin, then your positions will be automatically liquidated, and your account may be suspended.

- **PIP**. This is the term used to refer to the "points in percentage" that you can expect to see in the trades you make. Commonly, these points are referred to as "pips." These are relative terms depending on the valuation of the currency. In some cases, a pip may be equal to a penny. In others, it may refer to $1/100^{th}$ of a penny. It all depends on the relative valuation of one currency with regard to another.

- **Margin**. This refers to the amount of money you need to have deposited in your account. Some platforms require new investors to have a 100% margin. This means that if you deposit $100, you can only trade up to $100. If you have 1%, then you can trade up to $10,000. This means that you don't actually need to have the $10,000 to open a position valued at $10,000. All you need is to have the requisite funds deposited. However, if you should lose out on the deal, you will face a "margin call." In this case, you will have to pony up the cash to cover the margin call. Otherwise, your account may even be canceled.

- **Spread**. This is the difference between the buy and sell quote of a currency pair. The difference is expressed in terms of pips. For instance, is you have a pairing such as AUDCDN expressed as 1.17/04, it means that the upper and lower limits on the deal are 1.1700 - 1.1704. To break even, your deal must make at least 4 pips.

CHAPTER 2

Beginners Guide To Forex Trading

Getting started with FOREX depends greatly on your ability to master the various techniques that come along with it. This means that you need to be at least moderately proficient in computer skills. Having such skills will go a long way toward helping you quickly master FOREX trading, thereby helping you make money right away.

As such, it is important for you to become familiar with the software known as a "trading platform." A trading platform is a piece of software that you use as a means of accessing the FOREX market, therefore, allowing you to trade. You can get started with something as simple as a download. Of course, that is only scratching the surface.

It should be noted that mastering a trading platform requires a combination of study and experience. So, it's always best to make sure you have the right training prior to making your first official trades.

One very important piece of advice is to take advantage of the free demo account that comes with most trading platforms. If you are looking into a platform that does not offer a free demo account, then you might be better off searching for one that does.

The advantage of a free demo account is that you can play with monopoly money as you learn the ways of the platform and FOREX trading in general. You see, demo accounts are intended to give you access to the real market, analytics, and tools, but without actually putting your money at risk. So, you are simply running a simulation of what your real trades would be.

This is a vital part of your training.

By taking advantage of this, you can avoid costly mistakes. Since you are playing with monopoly money, you can make as many mistakes as you need to so that you don't actually lose out when you go live for the real thing.

That being said, we are going to discuss trading platforms and what they imply in this chapter. So, let's take a deep look at what you can expect.

Trading Platforms

Not all trading platforms are created equal.

This means that you need to do your research when it comes to choosing a trading platform. The main differences lie in the analytics and resources that a platform has to offer. You cannot expect a platform to provide you with everything you need if they are not fully transparent in what they have to offer. Moreover, the best platforms are the ones that offer you a demo account. That way, you can test out the platform for yourself before committing to any subscription plans.

In essence, any solid trading platform must offer you two things: access to all the trading tools you need and real-time analytics. These two elements will determine how useful a trading platform is, in addition to giving you the full range of tools you need to conduct successful trades.

It's also important to note that trading platforms should offer you both a desktop and mobile versions. This is key, as you may not always be sitting at your computer. Consequently, having the option to conduct trades, or manage your account, from your mobile device is crucial. This can enable you to move around, especially if you travel frequently.

Trading platforms usually charge you two types of fees. First, trading platforms charge a subscription fee. This could be a one-time setup fee or an annual subscription. Depending on the range of services the platform offers, this is what you can expect to pay. If you have a basic platform service that doesn't offer you real-time analytics and up-to-date information, then you can expect to pay a plat registration fee. On the other hand, if you expect real-time analytics and robust data management, then you may find that you will have to pay an upfront registration fee plus an annual subscription. The fact of the matter is that it's best to pay the additional fee because real-time analytics is worth every penny you can spend.

The second type of fee which you can expect to pay is a fee per trade. Most platforms will charge you pennies per trade. This is something which you must factor into each trade you make as these fees can quickly add up. Therefore, it's worth keeping in mind that finding a platform that doesn't charge you high trade fees is always a good option.

Also, please keep in mind that most trading platforms see bundles. These bundles offer a lot of trades, say, 10 trades for $1.99. These bundles are worth the expense as they can help you to plan your overall cost per trade, thereby allowing you to visualize how much you stand to gain.

How to Use MetaTrader 4

MetaTrader 4 is the most robust trading platform you will find on the market. It has been built to handle all of your FOREX trading needs. It contains everything from the trading platform itself to the robust technical analysis tools you need. This is why MetaTrader 4 is a great choice for your trading needs. Best of all, you don't have any hidden fees or upfront costs. In fact, dealing with MetaTrader 4 is rather straightforward. As such, you don't have to concern yourself with any unpleasant surprises.

MetaTrader 4 actually consists of several components. So, let's take a look at each one:

The MetaTrader 4 Trading Syste

The trading system is the main platform itself. It allows you to place the trades you want to place with virtually any currency pairing available on the market. Its robust capabilities enable you to put any strategy together regardless of how complex it is. This is what makes this trading system the most robust on the market.

It is also a very flexible and convenient option. It provides you with the best tools you need, such as market and pending orders. As such, market orders are the actual buy/sell orders you place as part of your trading strategy. Pending orders are trades that you can set up to be executed later on, for example, at a later date or under specific conditions such as a certain price point or trading volume level. In addition, you have access to trading charts, stop orders (including a trailing stop), a tick chart, and trading history. This is what makes the trading platform so strong yet flexible.

The trading platform allows you to carry out the following types of actions:

- Three different types of execution modes
- Two kinds of market orders
- Four types of pending orders
- Two kinds of stop orders including the use of a trading stop

These tools enable you to get any of your strategies up and running in short order. So, the only thing you need to do is put your strategy together so that the trading platform can execute it for you.

MetaTrader 4 Analytics

What good is a robust trading platform without the right analytics to back it up?

In this case, you get the analytics you need to set up successful trades every time. While the trading system is quite good, the analytics capabilities of MetaTrader 4 are even better. With it, you can access online quotes for up to 9 periods. Also, you can access interactive charts that can enable you to customize the type of information displayed. You can toggle the details so that they can reflect any price changes throughout a given period.

In addition, you will find a total of 23 analytical objects that include 30 built-in indicators that will simplify your trading tasks. This allows you to spend more time thinking about strategy and less time searching for useful information.

The analytics pack also includes the free Code Base app, which allows you to generate thousands of additional indicators. These indicators give you a wide assortment of analytical tools to help you make the most of each trade. The best part is that having a variety of indicators at your disposal enables you to make timely decisions as real-time data comes in.

With the analytics pack you will find:

- A series of interactive charts

- Nine different timeframes which you can analyze
- Twenty-three analytical objects to choose from
- Thirty technical indicators to help you make the most of your research

These are all included when you sign up.

Copy-Trading and Trading Signals

When you are pressed for time, you can simply copy-cat trades. Yes, that's right. With this function, you can copy-cat trades from other successful investors. This is the ultimate way to piggyback on great trades. Of course, you're not stealing anyone's hard work here. What you are doing is implementing a successful strategy. This is important when you don't have the time to sit down and craft your own strategies. This is a great tool, especially when you are on the run.

All you have to do is subscribe to any given signal. These are offered by specific providers. Some of them are free, while others are paid. The best part about using signals is that you can immediately put them to the test in your free demo account. As such, you can see which ones work and which ones don't. You can choose from various levels of risk and return. So, there is something for all tastes. If you want to play it safe, there are safer deals. If you want to run a bit more risk, there's that, too.

With this function, you can expect to find thousands of providers, thousands of trading strategies, and virtually all kinds of trading conditions you can imagine. Indeed, using copy-cat trading, you can quickly learn the ropes of FOREX trading from successful pros. Since there are plenty of free signals, it won't cost you anything extra to give it a try.

Using the MetaTrader Market

This function is quite interesting. It grants you access to an expert advisor. This means that you have access to any number of investment guidelines from real pros. You can purchase access to thousands of these apps, or you can choose free ones. They deliver useful advice which you can put into practice when designing your strategy. In addition, you can use them to customize your trading plans as real-time information flows in.

Also, you can search for the latest technical indicators. This is another great function as it allows you to detect which indicators reflect the best types of analytics you need to stay on top of the latest market trends. The best part of all is that you have a wide selection of both free and paid options. This makes it far easier for you to make sense of your trading needs.

Algorithmic Trading

This is where things get really interesting.

One of the core elements of successful trading is to conduct extensive market research. This is important as you need to be aware of the trends and latest updates on markets. This means that you need to be aware of what's happening.

However, this is not only time-consuming but also very tough to do, especially when you don't have much time. So, this is where algorithmic trading comes into play. Modern trading tools utilize algorithmic trading based on available market information. Then, an algorithm can be developed in order to reflect the trend in markets. The end result is a trading strategy based on the latest information and successful practices.

MetaTrader 4 allows you to integrate both algorithmic trading and Expert Advisor so that you can craft an automatic trading strategy. This implies that you can take much of the research out of trading while crafting a trading strategy that truly reflects the current information available in the marketplace.

This is what folks commonly refer to as "bots." The bots that you are able to create and automate your trades so that all you need to do is push the "trade" button, and the bot takes care of the rest for you. This is ideal for anyone who is looking to invest in FOREX but doesn't have a great deal of time to devote to research and trading.

MetaTrader 4 offers the following applications:

- MQL4 trading strategy editing language
- MetaEditor
- The strategy tester
- A library of free trading bots

Of course, if you are a bit more tech-savvy, you can develop your own trading bots. The neat thing about it is that your own bots can reflect your personal trading strategy.

Mobile Trading

MetaTrader 4 is designed to run on Android and iOS devices. This is the perfect complement to its robust toolkit, especially when you are on the go. For investors who are always on the move, having access to their trading platform on their mobile devices provides a great deal of flexibility. In particular, it allows you to keep up with the latest trends and information. Practically all traders who use MetaTrader 4 have their desktop application along with the mobile app. This is a great way of staying in the loop all the time.

Basic Forex Terminologies

In this section, we are going to look at three crucial terms that you need to become highly familiar with when trading in FOREX.

Price in Points

Price in points, or pips, are essentially the points that you expect to win, or lose, every time you enter a trade. In the previous chapter, we mentioned the function of pips and how you can use them to visualize the amount of money you can make per trade.

In general, pips represent pennies, or fractions of pennies, that you expect to earn on each deal. As such, pips are dependent on the cross rate between two currencies. If the cross rate isn't very large, then a single pip represents a greater degree of value than in a cross rate, which is rather extensive.

By the same token, pips are the standard measure that is used to determine the entry and exit points, as well as the various stop-loss levels in which you can set your trades. As a result, it's important to note that you need to keep the pip calculation in mind all the time.

The great thing about using a trading platform is that the platform does the math for you. As such, all you need to do is focus on the recommended pip points per trade. For instance, there are trading strategies that recommend leaving the trade after earning 20 pips. Don't worry if that doesn't make total sense at this point. The main thing to keep in mind is that your trading platform can take care of this for you. If you choose, you can also do the math yourself. In such cases, it's important to go over the data you are analyzing so that you can be sure that you have the most accurate and up-to-date information.

Lot Sizes

A lot size is the amount of currency you are going to purchase, or sell, in a given trade. The smallest lot size you can purchase in a single deal is one unit of a currency. For instance, you can purchase one US Dollar in exchange for, however, many units of the other currency you need. Additionally, there is no limit to the lot size, meaning that you could purchase millions of units of another currency. Nevertheless, this is not something that is customary as the average investor needs to be wary of their trading capital.

As for large institutional investors, they can really move the price action by purchasing massive lot sizes. These types of investors, for example, hedge funds, make massive deals in which they move millions of Dollars from one currency to the next. It's important to note that these types of investors engage in such trading for the sake of moving their money into markets that offer a greater deal of profit.

For the average investor, a lot size is important as it will determine the overall amount of money that will be invested in a single trade. In general, the golden rule of money management says that you should invest no more than 2% of your total trading capital in a single trade. As a result, you need to make sure that you don't exceed this parameter. Of course, you could invest your entire trading capital at once, but it just wouldn't be in a single deal. That drives up risk too high and could leave you bankrupt should something go wrong.

Limits and Stops

One of the greatest features of modern trading is the existence of limits and stops. Old school investors needed to be cognizant of the price action in such a manner that they could pull the plug on their deals before it was too late. This required investors to be glued to the ticker during the trading day.

Nowadays, this is not necessary. With automated trading, you can set up limits and stops to keep your investments safe. This is why becoming familiar with limits and stops is a must for every FOREX investor.

In essence, limits are used to set a point at which you will sell. Once the limit point is set, a sale order is triggered. The reason for this is that once the limit is reached, it is believed that the price will go down from there. Therefore, you stand to make less profit as compared to selling at the highest point.

Also, limits are used when looking to purchase. As such, limits are triggered when the price reaches a certain point. When that point is reached, the investor enters the trade. If the price point is not triggered, then the trade does not happen. That is why limits are very useful when it comes to setting up a trade based on the expectations that you want.

Stops are used to reduce the number of losses you are willing to accept. These points are also known as "stop-loss." They are quite handy when setting up your trades. A golden rule of FOREX investing is that you must always set up stops. The reason for this is that when a trade suddenly goes bad, you have a point at which you will exit the trade. This means that you cannot expect to continue in the trade at this point. Automated trading platforms have a function that is triggered by a "double stop." When you hit two consecutive stop-loss points, the system can be configured to automatically liquidate any open positions you may have. This type of configuration can save your portfolio from disaster.

CHAPTER 3

Setting Up Your Trading Platform

At this point, we are ready to get started setting up our trading platform. On the whole, MetaTrader 4 makes it very easy for you to get started trading. While you do need a fairly thorough run-through of the trading system, it's quite easy to get things rolling. This is why this chapter is focused on helping you get off the ground quickly and easily.

To get started with MetaTrader 4, you need to download the main software platform from the MetaTrader 4 website. This will download the installer pack, which then runs the platform on your Windows or Mac OS computer. Also, you can install MetaTrader 4 on Linux devices. As such, this gives you the flexibility to run this platform on any device you use. In addition, you can install it on Android and iOS devices.

The platform is available at https://www.metatrader4.com/en/download. So, do take the time to go over the system requirements to make sure that your device is fully equipped to run the platform. The last thing you want is to have your system crash because it doesn't meet the full range of specifications.

Once you have downloaded the MetaTrader 4 platform, you will be instructed to create an account. Simply enter your email address, and you'll be good to go. Also, you'll need to enter some personal information. This is standard stuff. At this point, you'll be prompted to choose between the full account and the free demo account.

Here is one of the most crucial investment decisions you'll ever make: choose the free demo account! You'll be granted access for 15 days. Do not forego the option to choose the free demo account as that would lead you to the full paid account. If you do this, you'll be trading directly with your own funds. In that case, you'll have to be very careful as mistakes can quickly add up and torch your investment capital. This is why the demo account is the best way to get started.

Later on, you can migrate into the full account. At that point, you'll have to provide a source of funds (a bank account or credit card) in addition to the various information items you'll be requested to fill out (mainly government regulation stuff).

Once you are on board with the free demo account, you'll have access to the full functionality of MetaTrader 4. Since there are no restrictions, you can get a great sense of what the platform has to offer. So, make wise use of your time. You can browse everything available to paid users. The only difference is that the winnings you make won't actually count. By the same token, if you miss out on some deals, it won't affect your account. In fact, if you get wiped out, the system will refresh your investment capital. However, there is a limited amount of times you can do this (two times). So, if you get wiped out twice, you won't be able to trade again until you actually top up your account with real funds.

One other thing: do take the time to go over the various types of views and displays. In doing so, you can set up the trading system so that it reflects your personal preferences and the setup you feel most comfortable with. Since you'll most likely be dealing with a great deal of charts and information, it's best to have a setup that you would feel most comfortable with. While some investors like to have a two or three-screen setup, MetaTrader 4 is designed to run on a single screen. However, feel free to customize it to suit your individual needs.

How to Use Trading View

Once you have MetaTrader 4 up and running on your computer, all you need to do is use ctrl+T to open and close the main window. Of course, you'll need to make sure that the platform is running. If you log out and end the session on your computer, you won't be able to use this shortcut. So, do make sure that the platform is currently running. The default configuration sets MetaTrader 4 to run on startup. So, it'll be loaded every time you turn on your computer unless you choose to do otherwise.

When you open up MetaTrader 4, you'll be set into "trading view." This is the default view for the platform. That way, all you need to do is open up the platform and begin trading. You'll have access to all trading features at this point.

Trade History

The "trade history" feature enables you to see the trades you have placed throughout your time on the platform. To access your trade history, all you need to do is click on the "Account History" tab. This tab is located across the top of the main window. Alternatively, you can right-click anywhere on the screen to reveal the drop menu. Once open, you can select the "All History" function. This feature allows you to visualize your entire trading history for the "last month" or the "last 3 months". Clicking on any of these options will display your history on the screen. You can also select to save your history data by clicking on "Detailed Report." This option allows you to generate a detailed report for your trading activity.

The great thing about this reporting feature is that it allows you to get information on the various aspects pertaining to your trades. Here, you view the price, lot size, execution time, profit, loss, and the date and time. This is highly useful as this allows you to review successful trades while also going over unsuccessful ones.

When you choose the "Save as Report" or "Save as Detailed Report" function, you'll be displayed this information on a new tab in your web browser. To save this information on your computer, click on any part of the screen on the hit ctrl+A to select all. Once the text is highlighted, all you need to do is copy and then paste on any word processing program such as Microsoft Word. You can then save the file directly on to your computer. This will also allow you to print a hard copy if you wish.

If you wish to display your trade history in chart form, you need to go to the "Account History" tab. Then, choose any trade by clicking on it and then drag it into a chart window. You will then see the trade displayed as a chart with the open and close levels marked in the chart by arrows. These two points will be joined by a dotted line to reveal the path of the trade. After, simply drag your mouse cursor over the line to see the information pertaining to those points in the trade.

Open Trades

To view open trades, simply open up the terminal. You can either click on the icon in the taskbar or hit ctrl+T. You can then view all open trades by hitting the "trade" tab across the top. All open trades are organized within the same window, so it allows you to visualize the action happening all at once.

Account Balance

To check your account balance, once again open up the terminal. Then, go to the "Trade" tab. There you will find a line that indicates your balance, equity, and free margin. At first, you won't have access to margin beyond a 1:1 ratio. As you gain more traction, the margin will increase. Also, you can request for greater margin.

Trade Level Colors

The default setting for colors for open trades on MetaTrader 4 is green for entry level and red for stop-loss and limit level. In essence, the green dotted line that represents the entry point of the deal is used to help you determine the exact point where you entered the trade. The red dotted line serves to indicate the exit point of the deal. This is also the take-profit point meaning that this is the point in which you would leave the trade successfully.

If you wish to change these colors to others which suit your preferences better, you can do this by going to the "Properties" tab or hitting F8. This will open up the menu in which you can customize these colors. You can choose from any of the colors available. In addition, you can also turn off these colors by going to the "Tools" menu at the top of the menu bar and then in "options" you can uncheck the box for "show" trade levels. This will leave you with a clean looking chart.

However, it is not recommended to turn off trade levels, especially when reviewing past trades, as this will help you to visualize the data in a much friendly manner. In the end, you can choose to customize colors to suit your vision.

Chart Background

All charts have backgrounds on which you can visualize the data. Most traders prefer going with a plain white background, as this gives you the easiest means of visualizing the data itself. However, you are free to customize this to suit your preferences. To do this, go to the "properties" tab or hit F8. Then, select the "colors" tab just as you did for the trade levels. You will find that the first item is "background color." You can choose any color from the drop-down menu. It's always a good idea to try out various colors so that you can decide which colors work best for you.

Working With Indicators

MetaTrader 4 is loaded with indicators. It comes pre-loaded with over 50 various indicators. These core indicators are set up automatically when you install MetaTrader 4 for the first time. For the most part, you might not see the need for additional indicators. The core indicators may be more than enough to meet your trading needs.

However, you might find that as you come up with more complex strategies, you'll need to work with an expanded set of customized indicators. This is important as your particular trading strategies may require you to search for more specific information. Therefore, you'll also need to make use of customized indicators.

So, we're going to be looking at how indicators work in MetaTrader 4.

On the whole, indicators are technical analysis tools that you can use to determine trends that you can use to support your models and strategies. These indicators can be used to provide you with reasonable assumptions about future price movements.

With MetaTrader 4, you get a number of indicators that are free. Then, you have a number of additional add-ons that are either free or paid, depending on the source. When you sign up for your demo account, be sure to check out which indicators are freely available to you. That way, you can play with them to see how they can help you make your assumptions.

Let's take a look at some of the indicators which you can use to help you visualize your trading activity.

Order History Indicator

With this indicator, you can go over any past trades while overlaying them onto any chart. This will enable you to recreate past trades using existing data so that you can determine if you are setting yourself up for success. Likewise, you can copy and paste other investors' trades and overlay them on any chart. This will enable you to see how the deal might play out.

Pivot Points Indicator

With this indicator, you can determine where pivot points may be located. For instance, you can set up a given pivot point based on previous market activity. This will enable you to determine where you might see potential changes in trend. Additionally, these pivot points can help you figure out if you are lining up a trade correctly. You can also set up alerts so that you are notified when a given point you have set up has been hit.

Hight and Low Indicator

This tool allows you to look up high and low points for any pairing on any chart in any given time period. This is great for when you are mulling over previous data. It enables you to determine when specific points were located within previous time periods. With the highs and lows, you can determine if your assumptions are correct or if you need to make any adjustments based on the historical data.

Trend Lines

These are, by far, the most popular indicators on any FOREX platform. Trend analysis is a fundamental tool of technical analysis. This indicator will allow you to visualize where the trends are moving for a given currency pairing. As a result, you can either play a trend -following strategy, or you can devise a countertrend strategy. The main idea here is to visualize both the trend line and the candlesticks for each period. Candlesticks are vertical bars that measure the open, close, and average prices during a given period. You can adjust these candlesticks to reflect hourly data, for example, or if you are looking at longer timeframes, you can look at daily data.

Chart Grouping

When you are working on multiple charts, this indicator works perfectly. What it allows you to do is to make changes simultaneously on various charts. This works really well when you are testing out a strategy across various time periods or with different currency pairs. You can group various charts regardless of the data contained. As such, it provides you with the robust capabilities you need to make the best of the data you have on hand.

Freehand Drawing

If you need to make customized notations, symbols, and other marks on any chart, you can select the freehand editor. This allows you to draw directly on the chart. You can draw your own trend lines, entry, and exit points, while also using various colors to highlight the information you are looking to make visible. Best of all, you don't need to have any special drawing tools. The indicator app allows you to do it directly on the chart.

Add-on Indicators

There are hundreds of indicators that you can add on to your platform. Feel free to browse through the free selections as they are ready for integration. However, the paid ones would require you to test them out first before committing to purchasing them. Among add-ons, you'll find stealth others, correlation calculators, task and alarm managers while also PIP calculators, and much more. Some of these add-ons are developed by some companies in order to promote their services, while others have been developed by fellow users who share them with all FOREX traders.

When you are working with the free demo account, make sure you give all free indicators the proper due diligence. That way, you know which ones you can incorporate into your trading strategy once you live. As for the paid ones, it's probably best to take advantage of any free trials before committing to your purchase. While they will do no harm to your portfolio, you might end up spending cash on tools you won't be using. So, it's always a good idea to test things out first before committing to a purchase.

Installing Add-ons

In addition to the pre-loaded indicators (which you can find by selecting the "navigator" window and then the "indicators" folder), you can install any of the indicators available to you. While you can search around for available indicators, your best bet at gaining access to virtually every indicator is through the MetaTrader Supreme Edition. This is a plug-in that is installed on the MetaTrader 4 platform. This plug-in comes in loaded with a host of indicators that plug right into your terminal. As such, you won't have to look around for them. This bundle offers a great combination of tools without having to break the bank. You can download it for free to test. After the trial version expires, you can choose to go for any of the pricing packs available.

Now, if you choose to install an add-on yourself, go to the "navigator" tab and go to "indicators." There you can choose the "browse" option to search the various types of indicators that are available for download. When you choose the one you like, you need to search for the MT4 data file. This file will be in your "downloads" folder. Now, select it and paste it to your clipboard. Once you are ready, go to the "file" tab and choose "Open Data Folder." This will open the "MQL4" folder, which then leads you to the "indicators" folder. Here, you can paste the downloaded file you copied to your clipboard. And, that's all there is to it! The new indicator should now appear when you open the "indicators" section of the "Navigator" tab.

Turning Off an Indicator

Once you have loaded your selected indicators, they will be active at the same time. This can make it easy to follow all of the action that you are looking to keep track of. However, there might be a case in which you don't want to have an indicator working for you anymore. In this case, to turn it off, use the crtl+I shortcut. From there, you'll be displayed a list of indicators. Then, you can select the indicator you wish to turn off. After, click on the "delete" button to make it go away. While this does not permanently delete the indicator, you will have to manually restart it if you wish to have function again. Nevertheless, it's a great tool to have in case you want to simplify things on your terminal.

Analyzing the Market

Being a successful FOREX investor requires a good dose of due diligence. This means analyzing the information that's available on the market. In a manner of speaking, it's like sports teams watching game film of themselves and their opponents. In doing so, they can be ready to attack the opposition when they take the field. Most importantly, it enables the team to develop a strategy that they can put to use when going on the field.

As such, market analysis is critical in the FOREX market. You cannot expect to be successful by simply placing trades haphazardly. You need to have analytics that can enable you to make the right investment decisions, given your expectations and risk tolerance.

The good news is that MetaTrader 4 provides you with a great deal of tools to conduct technical analysis. As such, you won't have to scour the internet looking for sources of credible information. However, it's what you do once you get that information that makes the difference between underwhelming returns and actually making money on deals.

So, let's take a look at three important elements of market analysis you need to become familiar with in order to become a truly successful FOREX investor.

Trends

Trend analysis is at the core of technical analysis in all financial markets. As for FOREX, it's vital that you become familiar with trend analysis as this will enable you to get a handle on where the various types of currency pairing may be going.

At a glance, you can quickly spot trends just by looking at a chart. However, the secret to truly analyzing a trend in charts is to spot the potential reversals in that chart. This requires a bit more of a trained eye as not all folks are able to easily spot these points.

Firstly, a bullish trend means that the valuation of one currency is going up with regard to another. When you look at a chart, you can quickly spot a bullish trend by noticing how the line curves upward, then rounds off at the top before beginning to descend. In some cases, you'll find charts moving up and then have a sharp decline in an inverted "V" shape. The goal, in this case, is to follow the trend so that you can get in before the price goes up and capitalize on the highest possible point at which you can exit the trade.

Secondly, a bearish trend is the opposite of a bullish trend. You can quickly spot a bearish trend by seeing the line dip down to the bottom of the chart in a "U" shape. If the recovery in price is quick, it will resemble a "V" shape. In either case, you'll find that getting out of a trade before the line hits the bottom is essential to either minimizing losses, or perhaps finding a potential entry point.

Lastly, when the line trades at a seemingly horizontal manner, then you are looking at a "sideways" trend. In this case, you are seeing how the currency pair is trading in a "band." The term "band" means that the pairing is in a tight range in such a way that there isn't much room to maneuver. When this occurs, it's either due to low trading volume or perhaps investors looking to get in at a specific point in time.

With MetaTrader 4, charts automatically calculate trends both in real-time and with historical data. This makes it a valuable tool when looking to make the most of the data you have available. If you are looking to trade with the trend, then it is quite easy to just follow the charts. If you are looking to follow a countertrend strategy, then you really need to pay close attention to any signs of a potential reversal.

Ranges

It is quite common for certain currency pairs to trade in a specific range or "band." In these cases, you have predictable movements in price. These movements are usually the reflection of investor sentiment when it comes to price action in that pair. Additionally, it is quite common to find that correlated pairs trade in a band. By "correlated pairs," we're talking about currency pairs that have a long history together. These are currencies that are commonly traded together. As such, there is a plethora of information on these pairings.

Consequently, investors know what to expect. Hence, they build strategies to capitalize on the range they trade in. Unless there is a considerable disruption in the market, you won't find correlated pairs suffering from any unexpected jolts.

Using the technical analysis tools in MetaTrader 4, you can determine these ranges as the charting application will show you the highs and lows. Over time, you can ascertain where these highs and lows can be found. Since currency pairs that trade in a range have a rather predictable fluctuation in their valuation, you can reasonably determine when to get in and when to get out. By following this dynamic, you'll most likely make money practically every time.

Significant Levels

In FOREX, significant levels are those which are charted based on the fluctuations in the pricing of a given currency pair. These levels generally indicate a reversal in trend. For instance, if a currency pairing is trading with a bullish trend, this trend will eventually hit a significant level at which investors are signaled to get out of the trade unless they risk losing money. When you set up alerts for these levels, they will quickly flash on the screen. This is where you can exit the trade manually or set up a limit in order to automatically liquidate your position when you hit that mark.

By the same token, if a currency pair is trading on a bearish trend, the significant level may be triggered to indicate that there is a potential reversal coming. When this occurs, the reversal may signal that it's time to get in. In such cases, you can capitalize on the upswing.

It should be noted that significant levels are also based on trading volume. When trading volume picks up, the system notices this. It then takes into account where the trendline would be moving based on the increased activity. This is important when considering that increased trading volume may be a signal that it's time to get out. If you happen to spot a high trading volume on the "sell" side, then it might be time for you to get out. In contrast, if you detect that a large number of investors are taking positions in a given trend, then it might be a good time to ride the wave.

So, do make sure that you set up alerts to notify you of changes in significant levels. This will help you spare yourself from complicated situations down the road.

CHAPTER 4

Taking Action In The Market

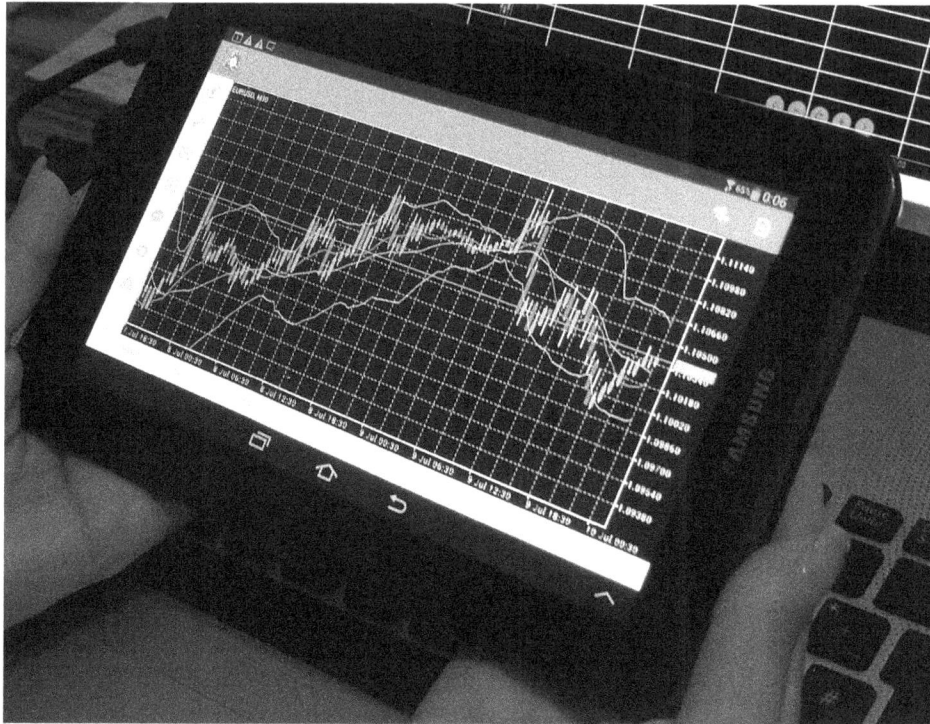

Now that we have covered the basics of the trading system and how you can begin to capitalize on FOREX trades, the time has come to begin getting our hands dirty. In this chapter, we are going to be taking a look at how you can begin to take action in the market. As such, you can begin to craft your initial strategies just as you would once you go live.

As a FOREX investor, it's important for you to understand the way that price is set in the market. As mentioned earlier, the currency market is ruled by the forces of supply and demand. This means that buyers come to the market along with sellers in hopes of swapping what each other is looking to get.

In a traditional market, buyers come loaded with money in order to purchase items that they need. In the case of sellers, they take their wares to the marketplace in hopes of obtaining money in exchange. In FOREX, you are essentially trading money for money. It may seem somewhat counterintuitive, but that's what you are essentially doing.

This is a clear difference from the stock market in which you are exchange money for shares of a company. Nevertheless, the FOREX market is highly liquid, meaning that there is an abundance of cash all the time. Therefore, you can reasonably liquidate your position any time you need money.

This isn't something which you can easily do with the stock market.

FOREX investors are keenly aware of all the various elements that influence the valuation of currency. In the section on fundamental analysis, we discussed how important political, social, and economic events are in the overall valuation of a currency. There is no question that all of these elements play a key role.

However, all of these elements need to come together at some point. That point is price. Price is the reflection of all the factors that determine the valuation of currencies in the market. Whether these elements are fundamental in nature, or whether they are technical, these elements all come together to produce an effect in price. In this case, price refers to the cross rates between two currencies.

So, this chapter is going to take a look at price action and how you can use this approach to help you define your initial trading strategy.

Using Price Action Strategy

In FOREX, "Price Action" refers to a discipline that helps you to determine how to conduct trades. While there are several tools such as moving averages that help to determine support and resistance levels, the fact of the matter is that price is the sole indicator that reflects any changes that may be taking place in the market. This is important to consider when analyzing both fundamental and technical data.

To capitalize on Price Action strategy, you need to analyze the trend in prices over a given period of time. This can be done with charts generated by your trading platform. These charts chart price movements based on the statistical tool called a "candlestick." Earlier, we mentioned that candlesticks are used to measure the open and close prices of a pair in addition to the average. This is important to keep in mind as longer candlesticks indicate a greater divergence between the open and close prices, while a shorter one indicates a narrower difference.

You will find the there are several indicators that are used to determine FOREX strategy. These include the MACD (moving average convergence divergence strategy), the RSI (Relative Strength Index) or the Stochastic Oscillator. These measurements look to model the movements in price. However, they are often inaccurate as they don't take the whole picture of what's happening in the price.

Perhaps the best indicator aside from price itself is the moving average as it charts the average price of a currency pair over a given period of time. The end result is a chart that plots the average price over a time period, thereby revealing the trend of the price of two currencies.

The RSI and Stochastic Oscillator are based on trading volume. Taking these measures into account as your main trading information can be deceitful as there could be any number of reasons for the increased trading volume. Therefore, the only true, accurate measure of movement is price.

The Basics of Price Action

To use Price Action strategy as part of your overall trading strategy, it's important for you to become familiar with price charts. As we've mentioned, your platform can generate these for you using any timeframe you choose.

To get started with Price Action, here are some ground rules to keep in mind:

1. When you begin testing out a strategy, it's best to stick to it for as long as you can. Often, investors make the mistake of hopping from one strategy to another. For instance, if you choose to use the MACD, then stick to it until you master it. This will enable you to get a sense of where this strategy will take you, particularly when considering the complexity of the elements involved. You will find that successful investors start out by mastering

one strategy. Once they see that it can provide them with good returns, they can move on to try out others. If it doesn't meet their expectations, they can try another.

2. Also, focus on higher timeframes when analyzing data. A timeframe can be a month, a week, or even a day. By the same token, you can analyze years of data. In this case, it's always best to analyze higher timeframes. For instance, you can look at the action over a month or more. This helps to eliminate any unjustified spikes in trading, which may convince you of unreasonable trading. This is important to note as sudden events may impact investor psyche, therefore, leading to a spike in trading. This is important to bear in mind as overtrading can catch up to you. By "overtrading," we mean placing too many trades in a short period of time. You might get sucked into this trap if you look at lower timeframes such as a week or just a couple of days.

3. Perhaps the easiest way to begin mastering Price Action is to copy successful trades. This might seem like a no-brainer, but it actually makes a lot of sense. When you copy successful trades, you can gain a sense of how to determine what to do in any given situation. As you gain experience, you will be able to set up your own strategy.

When starting out with Price Action, take a look at daily charts. Daily charts are a great way of spotting patterns. For example, you might find that certain currency pairs have a higher trading volume at certain times of the day. This may be the reflection of other markets opening and closing. Also, you may notice that certain price points trigger buying and selling. Thus, you can figure out where to get in based on these points.

So, let's take a look at some Price Action strategies which will help you get the most out of your trades.

Broken Trendline Retest Strategy

This strategy consists of assuming the behavior of a price will revert to the mean once the mean has been broken. This strategy plays off the fact that all prices eventually revert to their mean unless there are significant changes that can alter their mean. However, alterations in mean usually take a long time (relatively speaking) and do not happen overnight.

In this Price Action strategy, you need to plot a trendline for any currency pair. Generally speaking, the trendline should look into at least 20 time periods (usually a higher timeframe such as an hourly chart). So, you can take a look at the movements over the last 24 to 48 hours. This should provide you with enough information with regard to the overall behavior of the price itself.

Then, you can look for points at which the actual level of the price of the currency pairing breaks trend meaning it trades above or below the actual trendline. When this occurs, you can assume the price will return back to its original trend. This is where you can bank on profits being made. In addition, you can predict with reasonable certainty that the price will eventually shift back to where you originally spotted it.

To double check your strategy, you can go back to look at similar periods in which the valuation of the currency pairing broke the trendline. In such cases, you must study to see how long it took for the currency pairing to return to trend. In some instances, it might be a question of a few hours. In other instances, it might even take days. At the end of the day, it largely depends on the prevailing market conditions. Nevertheless, previous behavior should give you a very clear indication of what to expect.

You don't need any special indicators for this strategy to work. In fact, all you need is a price chart that contains at least hourly information. However, it is not recommended that you look at lower timeframes, such as daily data, as you could miss a great deal of information. So, a good rule of thumb is to take an hourly chart that goes back roughly 24 to 48 hours.

Resistance and Support Levels

To make the break and retest strategy functional, you need to focus on the support and resistance levels, as seen in price trends. Essentially, a support level is the lowest level that the price will touch down before rebounding back up. On the other hand, a resistance level is the highest point at which a price will hit before coming back down.

When looking at these levels, you can ascertain the band in which a currency pair is trading. Consequently, you can determine how low a price will go and how high it will reach. Generally speaking, you can determine these points by looking at the price action for the last 24 to 48 hours.

A good rule of thumb is to observe resistance and support levels, hitting at least three consecutive times. When you see this (the actual figure of a support or resistance level is always the exact same though it's very close), you can assume that any divergence of these support levels will mean a reversion to mean.

Let's assume that you are tracking the USDEUR pairing. You observe a support level of 1 and a resistance level of 1.05. This implies that the pairing will be trading in this range. During the period you are observing, you notice that the low point has hit 1, or at least very close to it. Once this point is hit, the price bounces back up to a max of 1.05. At that point, the price will come back all the way down to 1 and back up. When you notice this action for at least 3 times, you can assume that any time the price breaks through any of these points, you can assume a reversion back to mean.

So, here is where you can implement the strategy: track the price movement over a given period. When you see the price touch down to the support or hit the resistance level, then you need to be on the lookout for the price breaking either level. You can set up your trade so that it goes through as soon as the price breaks either point. Your entry point can be above or below the break while your exit point can be once the price reverts to mean.

A word of caution: be careful using this strategy when there is a high degree of volatility, as seen in wild swings in price or trading volume. In these cases, you may have unusual price action, which may take longer than expected to revert to mean.

Engulfing Bar Candlestick Pattern

In this strategy, we are going to be looking at the use of candlesticks as a means of determining price action and potentially identifying reversals. This strategy is highly useful when you are looking to track entry and exit points. Generally speaking, you are tracking price action over a given period of time in such a way that you are looking to determine where the price of a currency pairing will change trend.

There are two types of patterns, a bullish and bearish trend.

The bullish trend refers to price action that is going up. Therefore, you can expect the reversal to indicate a trend back downward. On the whole, you are looking to track the trendline as it hits the highest point of the resistance level. When this happens, the trend would be expected to revert down to mean.

The bearish trend refers to price action that is going down. As such, you expect the reversal to indicate price action moving back up. In general terms, you are looking to identify the exact point in which the trendline hits the lowest point of the resistance level and then changes course.

In both of these approaches, the candlesticks track the trendline indicate when the actual reversal has taken place.

To identify this exact point, track the trendline down to the lowest or highest point. You will notice a very short candlestick. The reversal official occurs when the next candlestick is much larger than the previous one. Thus, the next candlestick "engulfs," that is, it completely covers the previous one.

Let's assume a bearish pattern. In this case, you have the trendline moving downward. If you have been tracking the price action for any length of time, you may have an expectation of where the support level would be. As you observe the trendline moving toward the support level, you will find that the candlesticks are progressively getting shorter and shorter. Then, you will find a very short candlestick followed by a large one immediately following it. This is the reversal. This is the engulfing candlestick. This could serve as an entry point for a trade.

Now, let's assume a bullish pattern. In this situation, you are tracking the highest point in the trend. Thus, you are essentially looking to track an exit point. As the trendline approaches its highest point, that is the resistance level. You will notice every candlestick getting shorter and shorter. Eventually, the shortest candlestick will be followed immediately after by a much longer candlestick that engulfs the previous one. This is the official mark of reversal and should be your exit point. Ideally, you should exit the trade at the point of the shortest candlestick. This is the highest possible point you could achieve before your profit begins to dwindle. Of course, it's virtually impossible to track the exact point of reversal, but anything close to that point would serve well to maximize your profits.

Please note that most trading platforms use red-colored candlesticks to indicate a bearish pattern, while green-colored ones are used to mark a bullish trend. This color-coded system is very useful in helping you figure out how to spot reversals in trend.

Risk Management With Price Action

Risk management is an integral part of any kind of investing. When you follow tried and true risk management practices, you are able to hedge yourself from making mistakes that could wipe out your investment capital.

So, let's take a look at some risk management guidelines which you can implement when you are using Price Action as your main FOREX investment strategy.

1. **Beware of volatility**

   Volatility is the biggest enemy of the Price Action strategy. When you are using Price Action as your main investment strategy, it's important to keep in mind a high degree of volatility can lead to unusual shifts in Price Action. Since prices always tend to revert to mean, you can reasonably assume this will happen eventually. However, when there is a high degree of volatility, prices may return to mean faster or longer than anticipated. As a result, you need to keep your eye on this indicator even though it is not necessary to do so.

2. **Watch for false signals**

   There are times when you get false signals of reversals. For instance, you may get an engulfing candlestick well before the trendline hits the expected resistance or support level. While this is entirely possible, beware as it could simply be the result of unusual trading volume. If you spot a possible reversal well before expected levels, watch out for confirmation. Investors who jump in at the first sign may be in for an unexpected result.

3. Always seek confirmation

On the subject of false signals, always make sure that you get confirmation. If you see a potential reversal that does not fit the usual trading patterns, then it would be best to wait for a confirmation. Confirmation is needed to determine if there might be a new support or resistance level. Three consecutive hits can serve to confirm a new level. Some investors wait for only two hits before assuming there will be a third hit. If you are more risk-tolerant, you can go on two hits before assuming the third hit.

4. Be careful with countertrend investing

When you are starting out, it's best to avoid countertrend investing. The main drawback of this approach is that you anticipate reversals at points in which there may be no technical information to support this assumption. You can go on a hunch, or perhaps as a result of spotting engulfing candlesticks. Still, this is a risky type of investment that you must study carefully.

5. Avoid analyzing lower timeframes

When you are analyzing timeframes, always take higher timeframes. Most FOREX analysts recommend looking at periods of at least one hour. However, this would be too high. Ideally, looking at 20 periods, that is at least 20 hours, is the best way of tracking your strategy. In this book, we recommend looking at charts from 24 to 48 hours so that you can get ample confirmation of your strategy. On the whole, 24 hours is a good timeframe. However, 48 hours will allow you to filter out any price action derived from unusual trading activity.

CHAPTER 5

Price Action Confluence

When making use of Price Action as your main trading strategy, you can use confluence to devise your personal investment strategy. In the previous chapter, we discussed how you can use Price Action to determine entry and exit points for your trading strategy. In this chapter, we are going to look at how you can use confluence to set up your trading strategy.

As with all Price Action trades, it's important to keep a close eye on trends. Given the fact that Price Action is dependent on tracking price movements, setting up trades using confluence requires close study of price movements.

On the whole, confluence can be defined as the interaction between two or more levels. This interaction occurs within a single currency pair. As such, you need to be looking at the various levels of price action. For the purpose of this book, we are going to be looking at three specific levels: support, resistance, and trend. These three levels are what you need to track in order to determine confluence.

It is the interaction among the various levels, which makes the strategy work. When you identify the confluence of levels, you can determine entry and exit points, or perhaps spot signals for breakouts.

About Resistance and Support Levels

The simplest way to spot support and resistance levels is by spotting highs and lows. This is the easiest way to identify such levels without resorting to technical analysis tools. If you choose to employ technical analysis tools to determine support and resistance levels, you can get reasonable assurance that these are proven to be accurate. The way in which the platform calculates these levels is by comparing trend to the highs and lows of the timeframe under examination.

Just as we have discussed in earlier sections of this book, you can spot your levels by marking three consecutive hits on the levels you have identified. These consecutive hits must fall within the range. If there are breakouts or breakthroughs, then you need to be reasonably sure that they are within the range you are tracking. Be wary of points that break out of a resistance level as this could signal a new resistance level. By the same token, you need to be wary of price action breaking through a floor as this could signal a new floor. If you fail to spot this possibility, you could enter or exit at the wrong point.

An easy way to spot a new floor or ceiling is through the use of a "double top" or "double bottom." A double top consists of two consecutive hits above the resistance level you have identified. This is observed when there is a bullish trendline. So, you have identified three consecutive hits that you used to establish a ceiling. Then, you detect a hit above the resistance level, which then reverts to the mean. If the next hit pops above the resistance level, then you have just seen a double top. At this point, you can expect a breakout. When the breakout occurs, the third hit will rise above the ceiling. Therefore, you can reasonably assume that the new ceiling is now in place.

On the flip side, price action that breaks through the floor on two consecutive hits is considered as a double bottom. This is seen in a bearish trend. As such, the new floor is established when the trendline hits below the floor two consecutive hits. You can then reasonably assume that the third hit will fall below the floor. This could mark a great entry point if you are looking to play off the rebound.

During this analysis, confluence occurs when the overall trendline intersects the resistance and support levels you have identified. As such, the trendline will ultimately determine what you can expect moving forward.

Understanding the trend

To simplify things, use the charting function in your platform to calculate the trend line. Then, use the information reflected in the chart itself to determine the support and resistance levels. In particular, pay attention to the engulfing candlesticks to signal the reversal in trend as the currency pair trades within its range.

At this point, it's important to keep in mind that even though you have see-sawing action in the price movement, the trend line will ultimately determine if it is a bullish or bearish trend. As always, it's important to analyze charts that contain 24 to 48 hours' worth of data. Nevertheless, you can look at longer timeframes for the sake of spotting similar patterns.

Some investors like to take a look at a weeks' worth of data in order to establish recurring patterns. In such cases, it could be that the specific time window you are looking at does not reflect the trend in the market. While this is rather uncommon, it is possible that you are looking at a period that highlights unusual trading activity.

It should also be noted that trend is very short-term in the case of FOREX. Unlike stocks, FOREX investors live in the present, so to speak. Stock investors look at 20-day, 50-day, and 200-day moving averages. These are clear indicators of where the valuation of a stock may move. In the world of FOREX, things can turn on a dime, especially in times of uncertainty. As a result, you need to focus on the most up-to-date information.

Nevertheless, trend is clearly visible over longer time periods. So, it's worth analyzing longer timeframes for the sake of confirming your assumptions. Additionally, if there are relevant events going on in the world around you, it might be worth taking a closer look at trends well beyond the 48-hour period. It could be that price action was trending in one direction but suddenly reversed as a result of unforeseen events. In this case, think of events such as terrorist attacks, large company bankruptcies, or major political events.

Trendline Confluence

When trendline confluence occurs, you could be setting yourself up for an explosive gain (a breakout), or you could be heading down for a sharp decline (a breakthrough). Thus, understanding the points in which you anticipate confluence may set you up for success or save you from getting hammered.

In this section, we are going to look at three cases of trendline confluence.

1. Support level confluence
2. Resistance level confluence
3. Countertrend confluence

All of these cases use the trendline as the principal means of determining the trade setup while also ensuring that you enter or exit at the appropriate point. So, let's take a look at these setups in greater detail.

Support Level Confluence

In this type of setup, you are basically speculating on a breakout. Please bear in mind that you need to spot at least three hits in order to determine your support level. Additionally, the price action may reflect a resistance level, or perhaps not. It is not necessary to establish both a support and resistance level. The only requisite here is to establish a clear support level. In fact, if you see significant spikes, then you might be setting yourself up for a big gain.

Now, here is the most important part: the trendline needs to be located below the support level you have indicated. If the trend line is above the support level, you are too late. While you may still be able to ride the wave to the top, you can't expect to maximize your trade as you have gotten in after confluence, that is, the point in which the trendline officially intersects the support level. If you happen to get in right after confluence, you might be in for a big win. However, the later you get in, the greater your chances of missing out on the breakout.

To set up the trade, here's what you need:

First, clearly identify at least three points that indicate the support level. If there are more, then you are sure that's the bottom limit. This is the mark that you have a clear support level for the price action you are following.

Then, ensure that you have a rising trendline. This is important as a flat or falling trendline does not work for this case. If you identify the trendline emerging from a point in which there was a breakthrough, then you are poised for a significant increase.

Next, set your entry point at the expected support level point. This is the point in which you estimate the trendline will intersect with the support level. To simplify things, you can set this entry point automatically in your trade parameters. That way, the trade will only execute when the point is hit.

Lastly, set your stop-loss point at no more than 20 pips. This is important should the price plummet below the support level for whatever reason. Also, set your take-profit point depending on the risk to reward ratio you are using. For instance, if you perceive the gain to be massive, you can set up your risk to reward ratio at 1:3. So, if you set your stop-loss at 20 pips, you can set up your take-profit at 60 pips. This will lead you to a highly successful trade.

Note: if you exit the trade, but the price keeps rising, do not enter another trade. There is no telling the exact point in which the price will fall back down. So, it's best to sit out and what for the price to revert to mean. If you find that it doesn't touch the previous support level, then you might be seeing a new support level. Wait for a double bottom to confirm the possibility of a new support level and then repeat the same procedure.

Resistance Level Confluence

This type of trade is essentially the opposite of the support level confluence trade. The point of this trade is to avoid getting sucked into a falling price. This would not only zap your profits but may also leave you with a massive loss. So, it's best to make sure you have a good idea of what may happen.

In short, resistance level confluence is when you anticipate that a resistance level becomes a new support level. This is possible when the price plummets. While there is any number of reasons for this, you can use this type of trend to gain on the upswing. However, you are not anticipating that the price will go past the support level.

This is where you not only make money but also avoid getting hammered.

Here's how to set up this trade:

First, spot the support level of the price action you have been tracking. If there are multiple hits, then you can be relatively sure of this level. If there is a breakthrough with a reversion back to mean, then keep an eye on this as it could indicate a new support level.

Next, keep an eye on the original support level as this would be expected to become the new resistance level. This is due to the fact that the price will not necessarily revert to mean right away. Rather, it will hit the support level and then dip back down. This is the indication that the new resistance level has been hit.

Then, take a look at the trendline. Chances are the trendline will either be trading sideways (showing a horizontal move), or there will be a very slight upward or downward trend. If there is a clear upward or downward trend, then you are getting a false signal, as this could simply be an indication of volatility.

Lastly, follow the candlesticks. Check out the low point the price action hits before bouncing back up. When the price action hits the new resistance level and pops back down, you can set up your trade at the bottom and wait to cash in on the rebound.

With this trade, it's important to take care as you might enter the trade at what you observed to be the support level only to find that the price action broke through the floor. As such, you stand to get hammered. Please bear in mind that a sideways trendline is almost always a sure sign of this type of trade. Any other type of trendline will just be a false signal.

Countertrend Confluence

In this setup, you are working with a downward trend. As such, the main point here is to identify the resistance level as this point will indicate where you can expect the maximum profit to take place. Also, support levels are not particularly relevant. However, it would help to spot any double or triple bottoms so that you can ascertain where the low points may land. This can be used to help you set up your entry point.

Now, this setup is countertrend because the trendline is moving downward, yet you are looking to make money on the way back up once the price bounces back up off the floor. It should be noted that the platform will calculate a support level for you. So, a good rule of thumb in this setup is to make deals when the gap between the trendline and support level is the widest. This will enable a larger rebound. The shorter the gap between the trendline and the support level, the less money you stand to make. Additionally, you might be headed for a reversal. Thus, it might be best to sit this one out until you can spot the reversal.

To set up the trade, spot any double or triple tops. That will help you identify the points where you can expect the resistance level to be located. Then, look at the lows so you can set these up as your entry points. Last, set up your entry and exit points based on the lows and highs you have identified.

This strategy is quite useful if you are looking to make multiple trades in a single session. You may not get overwhelming returns, but this strategy will certainly help you get your feet firmly on the ground.

Stop Hunt Evasion

When investing in FOREX, it is always recommended that you set up stop-loss points in every trade. This is especially important when you are not planning to be at your terminal all the time. Some investors simply like to set up their trades and let the platform take care of the rest. That's why you need to set up stop-loss points on every single trade.

To do this, simply enter the price point for your stop loss below your entry point. Earlier, we recommended a stop-loss point of 20 pips. For instance, if your entry point is 10, you can set up your stop-loss at 9.80.

The reason for setting up a stop-loss below your entry lies in the hope that the price will rebound even though it has gone below your entry point. So, you can still capitalize on the upswing of the price. If the price does not rebound for any reason, you have cut your losses before they get out of hand.

Now, just as you have set up your stop-loss point, so has every other investor. You can assume that practically all investors have set up their stop-loss points within a reasonable level. This means that when the price suddenly plummets, a flood of stop-loss orders is triggered. This leads to a further price fall.

Some investors love to hunt for stop-loss orders in order to capitalize on lower-than-usual prices. This is called "stop hunting." To make money off this type of deal, you need to be keenly aware of the potential stop-loss points that other investors are setting up. Then, your aim is to capitalize on the stops so that you can catch the price of the currency pairing at the lowest possible point.

This is a highly speculative deal. This implies that you have no assurance that the price will rebound at the entry point you have selected. If anything, the price may still continue to go down further as the stop-loss orders continue to come in. Then, you might find yourself stuck in a position that's quickly falling in price. Then, there is no guarantee that the rebound will even get back to the entry position.

A good way of playing the "stop hunting" game is to play the countertrend strategy. Of course, you would need to be in the presence of a falling trendline (the stop-loss orders should reflect that). If this is the case, then you can expect a reasonable chance of the price rebounding at the support level for the currency pairing in question.

Stop hunting is not recommended for beginners. This is why you should first familiarize yourself with the various trend strategies we have outlined in this chapter. Afterward, you can make a reasonable assumption about the possible shifts in price so that you can set up your trades accordingly. While you can certainly make significant gains by stop hunting, please be sure to keep an eye out for false signals. These signals can be flashed when you see a high sell volume, but the trendline is moving upward. So, do keep an eye on the trading volume as this is the best indicator of a large number of stop-loss orders being triggered simultaneously.

CHAPTER 6

Introduction To And Rules Of Divergence

Divergence is one of the most common indicators which is used to guide investment decisions. When you are able to spot divergence clearly, you can pick up on the overall direction a trend is heading. In this manner, you can anticipate, within a reasonable margin, the potential reversal in trend.

When you go about using divergence as a means of setting up your trading strategy, it's important to note that you can profit from either a bullish or bearish trend. It all depends on how soon you are able to spot the potential reversal, as indicated by the trend itself.

That is why this chapter is focused on using divergence as a strategy so that you can set up your deals quickly and effectively. The main thing to keep in mind is that you need to spot the divergence so that you can take advantage of it.

In most books on trading, you'll find that divergence is determined by the interaction between trend and the moving average. This technique is commonly referred to as MACD (moving average convergence divergence).

In the MACD strategy, what you are essentially doing is spotting the points in which the moving average is going to intersect with the trendline. While this technique is highly effective, it may lead to possible false signals as the moving average is just one measure of what you can expect as a means of calculating the overall trend pattern of the currency pair you are tracking.

In this chapter, we are going to use Price Action as a means of determining divergence so that you can have a clear and accurate picture of when reversals are about to take place. You will find that this is the most effective way of determining divergence so that you can set up entry and exit points. Best of all, you are not using any additional measures beyond the most reliable indicator there is price.

When going about divergence as a strategy, there are some helpful tips to keep in mind:

- Make sure that highs and higher than the previous high and that lows are lower than the previous low. This means that when spotting divergence, your highs need to break out, and the lows need to break through. When you spot there, you'll be able to get the right tracking for the divergence you seek. Double tops and bottoms are the best way for you to spot this.

- Tops and bottoms need to be in successive order. This means that you must spot sharp dips and spikes. It won't work if you have smaller dips and spikes; all you might be seeing is an increased amount of trading volume.

- Ensure that the trendline is on the right path to intersect with the tops or bottoms you are looking at. Otherwise, you might be getting in too soon or too late. This is important as the reversal will take place at the point where the trendline intersects with a major top or major bottom.

- Also, please ensure that you look at different timeframes. If you focus only on tone timeframe, you'll be missing the entire picture. Please bear in mind that anything can happen in a short time period. So, it's always best to go back further in time to confirm your strategy. That way, you can be reasonably sure that you are on the right path.

Using Divergence for Entry and Exit Strategies

Divergence is highly effective when you are looking to plot entry and exit points as part of your overall trading strategy. Mainly divergence can signal at what point you can get in and at what point you should get out. It should be noted that the perfect entry point is the lowest possible point during a bearish trend. In contrast, the ideal point to get out would be the highest possible point during a bullish trend. In either of these cases, you would ideally get in or out right before the change in trend takes place. This is what can allow you to maximize your profit either way. So, let's take a look at how you can capitalize on this situation.

First, let's start with a bearish trend.

By definition, a bearish trend implies that the overall price action is trending downward. Even if you have significant spikes along the way, you can determine your trendline to be a downward slope. When this occurs, you need to spot when the trend will reverse.

The main point of playing a bearish trend is trying to determine the entry point of a trade setup. As such, you are looking to find the lowest possible point, right before the trend is about to reverse. Theoretically, this is the point where the trendline intersects with the lowest point of the price action. However, this point needs to be at least at the lowest point of the support level.

Consequently, the first step toward making this strategy work is to clearly identify the support level. A double bottom would be a great indicator that this setup will work effectively. You might try to go on a single breakthrough. However, that's not enough confirmation that the trend will reverse. That would constitute a false signal. Therefore, a double bottom is the best indicator. If you happen to see a triple bottom without the trendline intersecting, then you are getting ready for a huge takeoff.

Your entry point will be revealed when you spot the exact intersection of the trendline with the support level. This is where you can enter the trade. Then, you can expect the price to take off. The exit point is determined by your risk to reward ratio. You can set your exit anywhere from 20 to 60 pips above your entry. However, it would be recommended that you double check previous highs. This will give you the best indication as to where you can reasonably expect the high to hit.

Now, let's take a look at this strategy based on a bullish trend.

The whole point of this strategy is to figure out the best exit point. This exit point is intended to maximize your profit. Thus, the objective is to leave the trade at the highest possible point right before the trend reverses.

To do this, it's important to identify the resistance level. Ideally, you would have a double top you can use as a reference point. If you have a double top in which one of the points broke out of the resistance level band, then you may be seeing a false signal. This is generally due to increased trading volume. To make this setup work appropriately, you need to make sure that the double top stays at or very close to the resistance level. If you cannot spot a breakout after a triple top, then the downtrend will be quite sharp. So, it might be a good idea for you to set up your exit point slightly before the resistance level limit.

In both cases, it's important to automatically setup stop-loss and take-profit points as this will ensure that you don't fall asleep at the wheel. This is especially important if you don't plan to be physically present at your terminal. In such cases, the market orders will be triggered automatically once your specific point is triggered. Please keep in mind that setting up your take-profit and stop-loss points automatically will save you a lot of headaches further down the road.

Handling Divergence Drawdown

One of the biggest challenges that FOREX investors face when utilizing the divergence strategy is drawdown. Drawdown occurs when a number of stops are triggered at various points in a trading cycle. When a sudden number of stops are hit, the price may automatically tank, thereby leaving investors short of profit. In fact, sudden drawdown may trigger further stops.

This is why it's very common to find sudden dips in price. It's not so much that there has been a sudden shift in investor psyche; the fact is that when a number of stops are triggered all at once, the market automatically reacts. When the price dips and further stops are triggered, it can be hard to make a profit.

Unfortunately, some investors find that their positions are liquidated even before they get into take-profit territory. All of this is due to the fact that stops are triggered automatically.

Now, here is a common mistake that investors make: they decide to avoid setting up automatic stop-loss points in order to avoid being liquidated in a drawdown. This is a dangerous situation, to say the least. There is no doubt that you are playing with fire. It could be that the action gets hot and heavy, really fast. As such, you may not have enough time to react. This is why you cannot expect your human reflexes to react faster than a computer.

It's also important to note that divergence trading is not an exact science. Because of the fact that stops can suddenly be triggered all at once, you have to be aware that it is by no means a perfect strategy. This is why setting up your deal in the right manner will help you avoid getting knocked out of the game even before you have a chance to make a profit.

It should also be noted that you need to ensure to keep your instincts in check. If you choose to set up your take-profit points to high, you may not have a chance to get that high. As a result, you'll be knocked out by sudden drawdowns.

Now, there is one other thing to watch out for: if you get in at the bottom of the trend, it means that your stop-loss point will be much lower than that of an investor who got in after you did. As a result, managing an adequate risk to reward ratio will help you manage drawdowns much easier.

Consider this situation:

You got it right at the bottom of the trend, right before it reversed. As such, your position is now 1. You decided to set up your stop at 20 pips. This would set your stop-loss 0.80

while you are using a risk to reward ratio of 2:1. Consequently, you set your take-profit

mark will be 1.40 (20 pips * 2 – this is the 2:1 ratio).

Under this setup, let's assume that the price hits 1.41, then your position will be liquidated

as you hit your automatic take-profit mark. This means a successful trade. You make

money, and all is good. However, let's assume that you are feeling bold. You set up a 3:1

risk to reward ratio. This puts your take-profit point at 1.60. However, as investors get in

later, they set up their stops at around 1.45. A sudden dip in the price at around 1.47 causes

prices to dip below 1.45. This automatically triggers a bunch of stops. A number of

positions are liquidated, and the price does not make it past 1.40. Yet, you are stuck with

a take-profit point of 1.60.

Do you see why you may never hit your take-profit point if you set it too high?

This is why savvy investors know that it's best to set up trades that are realistic. If the

price of the currency pairing seems to be trending at a maximum of 1.50, for instance,

then you might be better off setting up your take profit point somewhere below this range.

This will ensure that you avoid setting up your expectations too high, thereby running the

risk of leaving you out in the cold.

Avoiding Divergence Drawdown

The easiest way to avoid divergence drawdown is to look at the resistance level for the

currency pairing you are tracking. While you might be tempted to set up your take-profit

point right at the top of the wave, you might think twice about it. If you see a double top, then a reversal might be upon you. In this case, it might be best to set up your exit point slightly below that mark. Even 5 pips can make a difference.

Another important way in which you can avoid drawdown is to anticipate it. You can tell a drawdown is on the horizon where there is a high volume of trading. If you see that there is a large number of trades happening at one time, you might be keen to keep an eye. If you see that the price has leveled off, sell immediately. The sooner you can liquidate your position, the greater the profit you will make. This is important as it will enable you to make a reasonable profit rather than see it get zapped by the sudden flood of stops. While this depends on your reaction time, it's usually a good way of avoiding your profits being zapped altogether.

Lastly, a good way to avoid drawdowns is to play it safe. If you liquidate your position well before the trend reverses, then you might consider re-entering the play, except this time with a much tighter position, say a 1:1 risk to reward ratio, just to be on the safe side.

How to Identify the Right Divergence Setups

Identifying divergence setups can be tricky. Thus far, we have gone over the main points that are needed in order to properly determine a potential divergence setup. So, it's important to go over the possible false signals that you may encounter when researching a setup.

The first false signal to watch out for is a trendline that does not figure to intersect the resistance or support level. So, you may have double or even triple tops and bottoms but no trendline to intersect. Now, you might be tempted to think that there might be a reversal, for instance, when looking for an entry point. However, you may find that a breakthrough is much likelier in a situation such as this.

Another false signal to watch out for is a trendline that is moving sideways. This is a very dangerous point to get into. If you are not careful, you might end up getting into a trade that will leave you missing out. When you have a sideways trendline, always be on the lookout for the candlesticks. If you see that the candlesticks are point toward a downturn, then be ready to exit. In this case, you may set up at a very tight stop and profit point, say, 10 pips either way. This is the type of setup in which you are looking to make a quick profit and leave.

Lastly, another false signal is when you do not see a clear trend. You may have double or triple tops and bottoms, but no clearly define trendline. In this case, the trendline may look like a wave or may have very sharps spikes and dips. This could be the result of an increased level of trading activity. It may just indicate that stock investors, for instance, are moving into FOREX as a means of getting away from stocks for a while. So, please try to avoid using the just tops and bottoms as a means of guiding your setup. You need to keep an eye on the trendline. Otherwise, you may enter a deal based on a false signal. While you may get lucky, the likelihood is just as great for you to lose.

Divergence and Confluence

Confluence occurs when two or more indicators meet each other at some point in a chart. This means that you need to look at various indicators to ensure that you have the right setup in mind. To do this type of analysis, the most common means is through the MACD.

In this type of strategy, you need to use the moving average of the currency pair you are trading. In this regard, the MACD will enable you to visualize the moving average of the price in question in addition to the price action. If you have both of these indicators moving together toward a point of intersection, then you have confluence. When they are moving away from one another, then you have divergence. Both of these scenarios are useful in helping you spot where your next move may lie.

Let's look at confluence first.

Confluence occurs when you have a price action trendline and moving average getting closer to one another. In the event that you have a bearish trendline and a bullish moving average, then you are seeing a potential reversal in trend. The reversal occurs at the point in which the two lines intersect. The point in which they ought to intersect should be somewhere at or near the support level. Once the lines have intersected with one another, they will begin to move away. It's important to watch out for the point in which they may hit the support level as the absences of clear bottoms may be more indicative of a breakthrough rather than a reversal in trend.

Now, let's look at divergence.

In the event of divergence, you have both the price action trendline and the moving average creating a gap. For instance, you have a bearish moving average and a bullish price action trendline. What this indicates is that the price action is slowing down. As such, it is a warning to avoid getting in at the wider points of the gap. If anything, you may want to look at liquidating your positions as prices may soon begin to level off. This would serve as a clear indication that it's time to sell. If the price action is getting closer to your take-profit level, just make sure you don't have any sudden drawdowns.

Using Bollinger Bands in Divergence Trading

Bollinger Bands is a trading strategy in which you have price action moving within a predictable band or range. This means that the price moves up to a resistance level and then falls back down to a support level before rising back up again. This type of trading is rather predictable and a great way of making steady earnings. This may not be the sexiest way of making money, but it sure is effective.

When using Bollinger Bands, the moving average is your best tool. You can track the trendline for the moving average in such a way that you can clearly determine the resistance and support levels. Consequently, divergence helps you to spot the exact points at which you ought to get in and the point at which you need to exit.

In short, Bollinger Bands set up both resistance and support levels based on successive hits on resistance and support levels. However, to use this strategy correctly, you need to identify at least three hits on both the support and resistance levels without any sign of breakout or breakthrough.

Additionally, you need to use a longer timeframe, say 48 hours, to truly identify this pattern. While this pattern is relatively common, especially among correlated pairs, it is important to note that the price action trendline will move up or down based on the moving average trend. So, your goal is to identify the exact point in which the reversal in trend will occur. At that point, you exit the trade, collect your profits, and then wait for the price action to move back down close to the resistance level and then back up again.

As stated earlier, Bollinger Bands are not the most exciting way of making a profit, but it allows you to make predictable earnings that you can count on to help you reach your investment goals.

Psychological Levels

For all the data and analytics in the world, investors are usually driven by psychological factors. These factors may range from fundamental elements such as economic stability to purely subjective factors like expectations.

As such, psychological levels are generally associated with resistance and support levels. For instance, investors may set up a round number as a particular threshold that must be crossed in order for them to buy or sell.

Consider this situation:

A currency pair has been trading in a predictable Bollinger Band. The price fluctuates from a high of 1.48 to a low of 1.41. As such, investors may not feel compelled to act out given the fact that there are very few incentives to make any large moves. This is due to the fact that investors see the 1.50 mark as a threshold. If the price moves past this point, they will sell. This would then trigger a flood of sell orders and knock the price back down. In contrast, investors will begin dumping their positions if the price falls through the 1.40 mark.

It should be noted that there may be no technical reasoning for this psychological expectation. However, investors have seen these round numbers, 1.40 and 1.50, as milestones that will dictate their ultimate reactions. This is why technical analysis should become your new best friend. Without it, you are left with subjective assessments that may have no real foundation for them. As a result, you might not make the best investment decisions. However, if your psychological perception is based on technical data, then you have a very good chance of making sound investment decisions and subjective assessments based on hard data.

Risk Management in Divergence Trading

Risk is an investor's worst enemy. Simply put, the greater the risk, the greater the chance you will lose money. This is why managing risk is so important when it comes to successful trading. On the whole, you can manage risk by paying close attention to the data. The more you study the data, the easier it will become for you to spot trends simply by looking at charts. Often, these charts will tell you everything you need to know. You won't even have to consult any expert advice. The combination of data, experience, and instinct will be enough to guide you.

That being said, here are some useful tips to keep in mind when managing risk.

- First, avoid committing too much in a single trade. Even if the trade setup looks perfect, it's always best to avoid committing too much money in one trade. The level of risk skyrockets the more money you put into a single trade. So, keeping the 1% to 2% rule in mind will save you from making a terrible mistake. This is especially important when you are first starting out.

- Second, avoid making deals based on false signals. Always look for all of the signs before entering a trade. If there is a signal missing or if you are unsure, then don't enter the trade. It's better to see you missed out on an opportunity rather than regret getting in. There will always be another opportunity.

- Third, play it safe. It is always best to err on the side of caution. If you find that the setup is perfect, committing 2% of your investment capital will be more than enough to validate your thoughts.

- Lastly, diversification is key. Most successful investors have multiple positions open in various currency pairs. This allows you to manage risk more effectively as you are not dependent on the action of a single currency. When you spread risk out among various currencies, you reduce the likelihood of missing out greatly. So, do your best to enter multiple positions in various pairs. That way, the losses from one deal can be offset by the winnings of another.

On the whole, risk management boils down to using common sense. When you follow the data and use your good judgment, you will find that missing out on a deal would be tough. You won't miss out on any good deals. Rather, you'll stay on the right side of your mistakes. While you will not have a perfect streak, the likelihood of you getting wiped out will be far less. That is why keeping the various guidelines provided in this chapter will ensure that you will come out on top more often than not.

CHAPTER 7

Risk Management In The Forex Market

When investing, risk is a fundamental factor that you need to take into account. If you choose to take on too much risk, you open the door for potential disaster. While that may sound a little over the top, the fact is that risk is a constant in any investment environment. As a result, it's imperative that you take the necessary steps to ensure that you make the best investment decision based on the information you have available at the moment.

Managing risk boils down to making sound investment decisions based on technical data. Whenever you base your decisions on subjective valuations, you risk making assessments based on incomplete information. This can lead you to miscalculate the circumstances under which you have evaluated your position. Consequently, risk management requires you to make a very detailed assessment based on technical analysis.

Now, it's important to keep in mind that if you don't have enough information to make an educated assessment, it might be best for you to sit out the action until you have enough information. As we have pointed out at various points throughout this book, it's best to err on the side of caution. When you strive to play it safe, especially in the early going, then you can be sure that you won't make any rash decisions that might put your position at risk.

That being said, it's also important to consider that if you have a higher risk tolerance, then it's worth considering that more aggressive moves require you to be even more studious of the data in front of you. Indeed, the large amount of data can be overwhelming at times. Nevertheless, it's totally worth plowing through the data. It's the safest way for you to learn the ropes of the FOREX market.

Earlier, we mentioned that MetaTrader 4 provides you with options that enable you to literally copy trades. With this option, you can study successful trades. In a manner of speaking, this is a type of reverse engineering which can allow you to make the most of the situation. Consequently, you won't have to struggle in the early going. You'll be able to see how successful deals are set up for yourself.

Ultimately, these types of setups can help you to identify your own setups. This is crucial as learning the ropes of the FOREX market boils down to ensuring that you have the right initiation. When you have the fundamentals down, the risk is reduced exponentially. By the same token, if you don't have any clarity with the fundamentals, then you are only asking for trouble.

That is why we are going to focus this chapter on the best way in which you can manage risk so that you can ensure a successful outcome with the majority of your trades. While we can't ensure that you will win every trade (if only that were possible!), we can ensure that you won't set yourself up for any catastrophic deals. This will help you build your portfolio to a point in which you will feel confident, making the most out of your trading endeavors.

Picking the Right Broker for You

Picking the right broker for you can be a daunting task, especially if you are not clear and what you should be looking for. On the whole, finding a good broker isn't too hard when you know what you are looking for.

However, the question begs: why do you need a broker in the first place?

This is a reasonable question. The reason why you need a broker in order to enter the FOREX market is that you, as an individual, are not officially permitted to trade in the FOREX market unless you have the backing of a licensed institution. In this case, the brokerage firms that offer access to their platforms are the institutions that will back your trading activity.

In a manner of speaking, it's like you're playing your home games in someone else's stadium. It's still your home turf even though you don't actually own the stadium. In this regard, the access you are granted to the platform enables you to place trades for yourself. All you pay to the brokerage firm is the right to use their platform.

That's all.

So, you aren't hiring a broker to manage your portfolio. What you are doing is simply "paying to play." A good way of looking at it is by comparing it to poker. When you play professional poker, you need to buy your way into the game. This is in addition to the blind you have to pay for each hand. Similarly, FOREX platforms will charge you for the access to enter the platform. Once you are in, then you can place your trades with the trading capital you have at your disposal. This will then enable you to make a profit.

The best part of this type of setup is that the profits you make are yours. You don't have to pay a commission to some broker for their "expertise." By reading this book, among other publications out there, you will gain the same type of knowledge that brokers have. Therefore, you won't have to waste your money by paying commissions. That goes straight into your pocket.

As such, there are some important points to consider when looking for a brokerage firm that can grant you access to the FOREX market.

1. **Membership fees**. All FOREX trading platforms will charge you some kind of membership fee. This fee is generally used to keep the platform running. Thus, the price you pay is what basically keeps the lights on. Regular brokerage firms will charge you a flat fee for the use of the platform. This can either be an annual fee or a recurring monthly payment. In other cases, discount brokers may charge you a one-time signup fee. However, they'll get you on the back end with their fees per trade. When you opt for a full-service broker, you'll pay a higher upfront fee, but you'll get a great analytics package that offsets the cost of the platform itself. Also, depending on the type of platform, you get algorithmic trading, expert advice, and even the opportunity to do copy-cat trading. Most discount brokers simply offer you access to the platform, and that's it.

2. **Fees per trade**. When you conduct individual trades, you generally end up paying a fee per trade. In some cases, you may end up paying a couple of bucks on each trade regardless of the size of the position. In other cases, you pay pennies per trade. The best way to maximize your value when it comes to fees per trade is to purchase bundles. Most platforms offer bundle packs like 10 trades for $1.99. These offer the most value as they allow you to control your expenses. If you go on a trade-by-trade basis, you'll find it hard to keep tabs on the amount of money you are paying per trade. So, it's best to see if you can lock in the price you pay for each trade you place.

3. **Reputation**. This is one of the most important aspects to consider. Sure, you might be tempted by the neat look offered by Joe's Trading Platform. But if you don't have any idea of who they are, you might be walking into a scam. The best trading platforms have a good reputation backing them. In addition, you'll find plenty of independent reviews on them by regular folks. You can even call up the Better Business Bureau in your area and get information on the parent company. Legit companies are always in the business of transparency as they know how valuable a good reputation can be.

4. **Free demo account**. This is a deal-breaker. If a platform does not offer you a free demo account, then it's better if you pass on them, at least in the early going. When you don't have access to the free demo version, then you will be playing for real right from the start. This can be dangerous, particularly when you don't have a lot of experience. So, a demo account will always be your best bet. Most platforms will require a credit card number or some other type of payment option though they won't bill you until after the trial period has ended. Take full advantage of this time as you are playing with house money. Therefore, you can afford to make a few mistakes. That way, you know what to look out for when you live with the real thing.

Please keep these points in mind as they will save you a lot of headaches along the way. In particular, ensuring that you are dealing with a reputable company is the most important thing you can do to protect yourself from unnecessary risk.

Signs of a Legitimate Broker

When you are selecting the brokerage firm you plan to do business with; there are a number of signs you can look out for. So, let's take a look at these signs:

1. You can get full information on the parent company running the platform. This is a biggie. If you cannot find out who's behind the platform, then you are better off staying away from them. When you know who is running the show in the background, then you can rest assured you are dealing with pros. The main issue to keep in mind is that not being sure of who you are dealing with can lead you to give your money to unlicensed firms. This will not only result in you losing your money, but you may also end up sharing sensitive personal information.

2. They are licensed. This is another important thing to consider. If the firm you are dealing with cannot produce any official licensing information, then you had better run away as fast as you can. Please keep in mind that platforms pop up every so often. Now, they might be licensed for a while. But after the scam enough people, they lose their licensing. Yet, they advertise themselves as if they were duly licensed. So, a cursory check at their licensing information should provide you with the assurance you need. In particular, a walk through the Securities and Exchange Commission's (SEC) website should provide you with the assurance you seek.

3. The price makes sense. When you are dealing with officially licensed firms, the price will reflect this. While we're not saying that it will be expensive, we are saying

that the price will be on par with the market. This is why you need to beware of prices that are too good to be true. Of course, there is always the chance that you are dealing with promos. However, the price should be a major tip-off.

4. There are plenty of reviews about them. Whether they are good or bad, you will find a good number of reviews about them. Users will be happy to leave both good and bad comments if given a chance. As such, finding a good amount of comments about them will help you determine if they are right for you. In contrast, if you can't find any information on them, then you might very well be dealing with a fraudulent company. This is why user feedback is so important.

5. They have an active presence on social media. If they are legit, you'll find them all over social media. Consequently, you will also find a number of user reviews and conversations about them. This is a great way of knowing who you're really dealing with. Even if they are new in the market, you'll them making an effort to gain traction on social media. In some cases, legitimate brokers will go out of their way to ensure engagement. Such efforts are always a positive sign.

Signs of an Illegitimate Broker

When you're shopping for a brokerage firm to grant you access to the market, it might be tempting to go with the cheapest option you can find. At first, this may seem like a good idea, but one the whole, please bear in mind that you get what you pay for. So, here are the most important signs to watch out for when looking to spot illegitimate brokers.

1. They don't offer a demo account. This is a key issue when it comes to determining if you are dealing with a legit broker. Any time you sign on for a new account, you should get a chance to try out the platform for free during a short trial period. This period is generally 15 days though it could be longer depending on the type of promotion the company may be running. In some cases, you may get a full access 7-day pass. As long as you get the free trial period, you can rest assured that you'll have the chance to test the entire system out first and then make up your mind. If the broker asks for money upfront, then you may be getting yourself in trouble.

2. They don't disclose their licensing information. This is an automatic deal-breaker. If you can't get any information on their licensing, then it's best to just get away from their platform. Clever scammers may appear to sell you access to a platform, but you might find out that it's just a test platform or some other type of demo software that doesn't actually trade the real thing. So, you might get scammed into believing you are really trading when you're really not. Also, you may be dealing with a once reputable broker that either has an expired license or a revoked one. So, make sure you do your homework on this one.

3. They don't provide any information about their leadership or board members. When you're dealing with legitimate companies, they are generally publicly traded firms. As such, this type of information is available on their website. You can easily find out who's on their board and what type of credentials they have. Additionally, you can find links to social media pages like LinkedIn. While this isn't exactly a

guarantee either, illegitimate brokers are usually scant with the amount of information they provide.

4. You can't find information on the financial institution backing them. Whether it's a financial institution such as an investment firm or a bank, you'll be able to easily get information on who's running the platform. If the platform is not clear about this, they are trying to scam you, plain and simple. By getting information on the institution supporting the platform, you can then decide if you'd like to do business with them or not.

5. They are little to no reviews. Some of them are clearly fake, too. Social media is really good at exposing scammers. If you find that their social media sites are filled with glowing reviews, that should serve as a red flag. Additionally, it's important to keep in mind that there will always be unhappy folks. So, a balanced amount of positive and negative comments should provide you with enough food for thought. Also, if positive comments appear to be coming from fake profiles, then you have an idea of what you're dealing with.

Money Management in FOREX Investing

Learning about money management in the world of FOREX is an essential tool that will help you steer clear of trouble. Mainly, money management pertains to a set of principles that you can apply when making investment decisions. These rules enable you to build a discipline that can help you to protect your investment capital while maximizing your potential for profit and gain.

So, here are 10 rules which can help you make the most of your investment dollars in the FOREX market.

1. **Stay clear of any software, programs, or platforms that guarantee results**. This goes without saying. Nothing is guaranteed in life. Yet, you will find that there are programs and companies that tout their platforms, programs, systems, and so on as guaranteed money-makers. The only thing that can guarantee you solid results is good, old-fashioned study and dedication to trading. Please be careful as so-called gurus and experts may offer you the keys to the kingdom for a low price. These are generally scams that, in the best of cases, will only leave you with subpar results. So, please be wary of any trading system that offers amazing returns in a short time period.

2. **Make use of a demo account**. Any reputable FOREX platform will offer you a free demo account loaded with monopoly money. Make sure that you take full advantage of this account. Not only will it help you to learn the ropes of the platform itself, but you can also practice as much as you can without the worry of losing any real money. If anything, you can go wild and try out any number of strategies before going live. There is no better way for you to learn how to trade without the risk of losing your initial investment. We have mentioned this point several times. It is so important that it's part of the rules of money management.

3. **Avoid involving emotions**. This is arguably the most important rule. The reasoning behind this rule is that getting emotionally involved can backfire on you.

Whether you are winning or losing, when emotions get the best of you, you open up yourself to taking on risk you normally wouldn't take. So, if you are upset after losing out on a deal, it might be best to push back from the table and take a break. There is nothing with catching a breather, especially when things aren't going your way. Please remember that keeping a level head when trading in any market is one of the cornerstones to making sound investment decisions. Sure, we are all human and get emotional. But if you let your emotions dictate your strategies, then you might be setting yourself up for trouble down the road.

4. **Don't be stingy on a good education**. When it comes to studying FOREX, don't cut corners with your time and your efforts. You don't have to spend a great deal of money. All you need is to invest time and effort into learning as much as you can about investing in FOREX. Most importantly, please keep in mind that this is an ongoing process. Books such as this one, are a valuable means of improving your trading acumen. There are also other publications that you can provide you with information that can be useful at any given point. Additionally, there are training courses out there which you can take on major learning platforms. These courses are not endorsed by any specific platform or broker. So, you can be certain that you are going to receive unbiased information.

5. **Being successful at FOREX is something that you can learn**. Being successful at FOREX isn't something that you can just pop out of a box. While it takes time to master the market, it is something that you can totally learn. That is why no system can guarantee to be foolproof. While you can use systems out there

as a guide, you need to take the time to make sure it's the right system for you. Please keep in mind that all skills are learnable. If you have the chance to learn from experienced pros, so much the better. The main point here is to make learning a lifelong journey. You will find that there is so much more to learn in the world of investing. In fact, don't be surprised to find that when you thought you knew everything there was to know, something else comes up that expands your current knowledge base.

6. **Manage your funds wisely**. A good rule of thumb is to never invest more than 2% of your investment capital on a single deal. When you do this, the problem is that it opens up the door to a great deal of trouble. For example, if you go all-in on a single deal, you run the risk of blowing your entire capital. This would not only be devastating, but you would be broke afterward. Please take care of your investment capital as much as possible. Even if you are just starting out with a few hundred dollars, your investment capital is highly valuable. So, blowing it all irresponsibly makes no sense. The 2% rule is an iron law that will help keep you in the race all the time.

7. **Spread the wealth**. While you might feel comfortable trading certain currencies, it's important to branch out and explore other potential currencies. You might be surprised to find that there is money to be made in various types of currencies. Often, most investors overlooked hidden gems such as those countries whose currency is gaining value. This is why fundamental analysis is always a great way you can sniff out a potential deal. Please keep in mind that diversification is the

name of the game. This is especially true when you're dealing with uncorrelated pairs. You will find that these pairs offer the best hedge against the risk that comes with putting all of your eggs into a single basket.

8. **Common sense always wins**. When you look at potential deals, or experts claiming to have magical formulas to great returns, use your common sense. This is especially true when you think about something being "too good to be true." In such cases, common sense would dictate a more cautious approach. In addition, if you have a gut instinct telling you that something is not right, it's always best to err on the side of caution. If you find that the data just doesn't seem to back your assumptions, then you might be better off sitting on the sidelines. In FOREX, it's better to prove yourself that you were right, even though you didn't get into the trade as opposed to getting in just to find out you were wrong. The good part about sitting out is that you then have experience which can serve later on.

9. **Hedge risk as much as possible**. The use of stop-loss orders must become your new go-to device whenever you enter a deal. The use of stop-loss orders will cap your losses up to a certain point. This will keep you from being wiped out in case a deal should happen to go sour at any point. This is why we keep reminding investors over and over about the importance of implementing stop-loss and take-profits points all the time. You might be tempted to take the auto-pilot off and fly solo, but please bear in mind that action can get hot and heavy. As a result, you may not have enough time to react. As such, you may end up losing out simply because you didn't react fast enough.

Take care of overusing leverage. This is another one of those risky strategies that you need to keep in mind. When you make heavily leveraged deals, you are opening the door for disaster. So, make sure that if you do use leverage, you have found a manageable level that would ensure you don't get wiped out should something not go right.

With these golden rules, you will come out ahead most of the time. While there are no guarantees in any market, you can be sure that you will have a good chance to come out ahead every time. So, do take the time to go over these rules again and again until they become second nature to you. In the end, you'll find that the combination of theory and practical experience will help you build the killer instinct you need to be successful in the FOREX trading market. Ultimately, all the skills you need are perfectly learnable. Thus, please devote as much time as you can to learning and building upon your current skills.

CHAPTER 8

Analysis & Trade Sharing

In the rule of money management, we mentioned investor psychology as a crucial factor to consider. Indeed, your mentality plays a critical role in establishing a winning attitude during your trading activities. Those investors who are able to keep their emotions in check are the ones who can maintain a more balanced approach. Those who cannot keep their emotions in check often find themselves making deals they later regret.

Let's consider an example of this situation.

When you make a bad deal and lose money, you might be tempted to "double down." When you double down, you are essentially going "double or nothing." Needless to say, the risk that's involved in this type of deal grows exponentially the more you double down.

Now, it's one thing to lose $100 and double down on that. However, if you lose $100, then lose $200, double down on $400, and so on, you are taking on completely unnecessary risk. Unless $100 represents 1% of your investment capital, it's best to let it go. You will be able to offset those losses with the profits you make from other deals.

In fact, when you double down, you are increasing the likelihood of failure exponentially.

How so?

Please take a look at the following chart:

Investment Capital	% Lost	$ Lost	Remaining Balance	% Gain Required to Break Even
$1,000	-5.00%	$50	$950	5.26%
$1,000	-10.00%	$100	$900	11.11%
$1,000	-20.00%	$200	$800	25.00%
$1,000	-30.00%	$300	$700	42.86%

$1,000	-40.00%	$400	$600	66.67%
$1,000	-50.00%	$500	$500	100.00%
$1,000	-60.00%	$600	$400	150.00%
$1,000	-70.00%	$700	$300	233.33%
$1,000	-80.00%	$800	$200	400.00%
$1,000	-90.00%	$900	$100	900.00%
$1,000	-95.00%	$900	$50	1,900.00%

In this chart, we can see how the more money you put into a trade, the more money you need to double down in order to recoup your losses. So, if you start off with a $1,000 investment and lose $50 of it, you only need to profit 5% in your next deal to make your money back. However, if you were to invest half of it, that is $500, you would need to double your money on subsequent deals in order to break even. If you invest $900, you need to make a 1,900% profit just to make your money back. Naturally, this is an unrealistic amount of money to make. You might be able to make that type of return over a series of successful deals (rather tough, though not impossible). Ultimately, this is not the best strategy to keep in mind.

As you can see, this is why keeping your emotions in check is a valuable tip you can put into practice. If you let greed get the better of you, you may not be able to recover from a mistake. By the same token, if you get sucked into the doubling-down game, you may not be able to pull yourself out of the hole. Moreover, if you decide to double down using leverage, you may very well end up getting banned from the platform if you are unsuccessful.

Now, you might be thinking, "what if I am successful?"

That is a very dangerous situation. It could lead to a false sense of security. You might think you are really smart when you were just lucky. Of course, we are not doubting your skills and intelligence. However, doubling down on a deal is so risky. It can lead to any number of possible situations in which you risk losing your entire investment capital. As a result, it's always best to err on the side of caution. You never know what can happen. Thus, it's best to be on the safe side, especially in the early going.

Developing a Solid Trading Mindset

Throughout this book, we have emphasized the importance of solid technical analysis and objective data. However, a good mindset is just as important. This implies that having a good mindset can be just as important as maintaining a close watch on the technical data that you need to place successful trades.

Often, novice investors get sucked into a silly game. This game consists of the Hollywood version of what an investor should be. Many times, Hollywood films depict investors and brokers as overly aggressive individuals who are arrogant and egocentric. Moreover, these films make it seem like you have to be pushy and go to extremes to make money.

What these films don't generally depict is that becoming a successful investor or broker isn't about being the toughest or meanest kid on the block. Being a successful investor is about learning to take your lumps in stride while using your head to make sound investment decisions. When you are able to make decisions based on reliable data, you can filter out the negative emotions that come with investing.

What negative emotions are we talking about?

Here are some to consider:

- **Fear**. This is by far your biggest enemy. Fear can compel you to act irrationally while also cause you to freeze. For example, when the market is a sudden downturn, investors panic and begin dumping their positions. This leads to bargains that can be scooped up later. So, a good rule of thumb to consider is that when others are liquidating their positions, look for bargains you can scoop up. Who knows what goodies you can find on the cheap?

- **Greed**. It's easy to fall for greed when you have a string of successful trades. You might go on a roll and make a killing. This can lead to a false sense of security. You might even think that you have it all figured out. And while that may be true, the problem lies in the fact that you take on unnecessary risk. Herein lies the problem. If you think you have everything down cold and decide to take on more and more risk, you are simply opening up the door to trouble. So do make sure that you keep in mind the fundamentals that have made you successful in the first place.

- **Anger.** This is another emotion that is hard to keep in check. When you get upset over anything, you might be tempted to act out irrationally. Simply put, if you are angry or upset over any unsatisfactory issues, then you might be better off simply sitting out a few rounds until you calm down. Believe it or not, hasty decisions can end up killing any progress you have made.

- **Desperation.** Unfortunately, some investors get into the FOREX market out of sheer desperation. They are in a dire financial situation. This leads them to pin their hopes on investment opportunities like FOREX to save the day. This can then lead to unrealistic expectations. When these folks see that money doesn't just fly out of the computer screen, they become increasingly desperate to make returns happen. This is where such folks are willing to take on unnecessary risk. They may be perfectly willing to go all-in hoping to hit a home run. In the end, they may very well hit that home run. But along the way, who knows what can happen.

The best way to offset this type of mentality is to maintain reasonable expectations. Sure, we all dream of scoring a huge hit that can suddenly make us wealthy, the fact of the matter is that the likelihood of such deals happening is once in a lifetime. So, setting up realistic expectations will help you keep your mind in check.

To set realistic expectations, think about the average return in the FOREX market. This is generally around 6% to 8%. When you look at the grander scheme of things, that's a pretty solid return. For the sake of simplicity, let's say that you earn 5% on average on every successful trade. That's money that can quickly add up.

Naturally, this type of return won't make you a millionaire overnight. But if you are prepared to be patient, you can earn a decent income out of trading. This is the best means of supplementing your income. Again, you might not become an overnight millionaire, but you'll at least put yourself in an incredible position down the road.

Another important aspect to keep in mind when managing your mindset is to have a clear goal in mind. If you are thinking, "I want to quit my job by the end of the year," you might be aiming a bit too high. However, if your plans are to put an extra couple of hundred bucks at the end of the month, then you have set yourself an attainable goal.

Let's consider how you can set a realistic goal in this regard: you start off with $500. Now, let's assume that you place 10 trades in a day. Let's go with the law of averages, so let's say that you'll win 5 trades and lose 5. This puts you at a 50% effectiveness rate. If you invest 2% of your investment capital in these 10 trades, you are investing a total of $100. At a 5% profit rate, you are making $5. If you keep your losses to a 5% average, you would break even.

The previous example may not seem particularly overwhelming. But if we upped the winning percentage to say 7 out of 10, then you are making the same 5%. However, you would only be losing about $2. All of a sudden, you have made a profit of $3.

For the sake of simplicity, this example highlights how you can make modest but solid returns. If we were to multiply these returns over a larger number of trades, you could potentially multiply $3 a hundred times over. This is where you begin to see solid returns.

Please note that making money on FOREX is a numbers game. As a result, the more successful trades you make, the more money you stand to earn. This differs greatly from trading stocks. In stock, you can hold on to a stock for months and clean up when the stock shoots through the roof. In FOREX, the longer you hold on to a position, the greater the likelihood you'll lose money. Hence, it's always best to liquidate your position as soon as you hit your take-profit point.

Don't Quit Your Day Job

One of the biggest motivators driving investors to get into the FOREX market is to achieve financial independence. This is certainly a reasonable goal to have. However, if you have your heart set on quitting your day job to become a full-time investor, then there is something you should know.

Full-time investors essentially trade their day job to spend the bulk of their productive hours pouring over charts and data. This means that you really need to be engaged with the prospect of investing in order to make this a career basically. If you only have a passing interest in FOREX, then it might be best for you to reconsider leaving your current employment.

When thinking about setting realistic expectations for your investment strategy, considering your FOREX endeavors as a means of supplementing your income is ideal. When you look at investments like FOREX as a means of giving you the extra income you need to pay debts and set yourself on the right track for financial freedom, you give yourself the breathing room you need.

In addition, when thinking about financial freedom, you are looking for the most important thing that we all search for: free time. Yes, financial freedom allows you to do with your time what you wish. This implies that having a steady stream of additional income will enable you to eventually take ownership of your time. Consequently, you won't have to be in the rat race your entire life. You will be able to make the most of your time with your family or any other activity you wish to engage in.

Another important consideration when it comes to investing is generating what is known as passive income. The term "passive income" means that you have income that you don't "work" for. Now, most folks confuse passive income with getting money for nothing. Please be advised that there is no such thing.

To generate passive income, you generally have to work a lot upfront before letting the source of income sit. Meanwhile, it is generating income for you while you only maintain it. This is the definition of passive income. When you work hard at learning FOREX, you will be able to generate enough trading strategies which can generate a steady income for you. As such, all you have to do is set them up and let them do the work for you.

That's all it takes.

Before you know it, you'll be making a decent living. On top of that, if you live a rather frugal lifestyle, you'll be sitting comfortably far sooner than you could have ever imagined.

Lastly, FOREX investing enables you to set up multiple income streams.
One of the pillars of financial independence is having multiple income streams. This term refers to setting up multiple sources of income that you can tap into throughout the month. This enables you to gain true independence as you don't
depend on just one source of income.

This is what allows you to achieve true freedom.

You see, when you don't depend on a single source of income, you are not overly concerned about what may happen if you lose one income stream. Should the worst happen, you can go on a replace a lost stream. However, when you depend on just one source of income, any sudden loss of that source will most likely destroy your finances. This is why having multiple sources is the most important thing you can do to ensure that you are on the right track.

Additionally, FOREX trading is the type of activity that you can integrate into your regular routine. This implies that you can easily incorporate your FOREX trading activities into your schedule. Sure, that might mean spending some time in the evenings or weekends at your computer. But please bear in mind that its part of that upfront effort that will end up paying off in the end. By the time you have achieved true mastery of the FOREX market, you'll be able to make trades easily and without much hassle.

Of course, there is one thing to consider though: never take your eye off the ball. So, even if you fully automate your trades, it's still important to make sure that you don't completely disconnect. By keeping tabs on the market, you can be sure that you will be able to handle any situation which may arise.

Maintaining a Healthy Body and Mind

An often-overlooked part of being a successful investor is staying healthy. It might not seem like it on the surface, but when you really think about it, it's important to balance every aspect of your life. Generally speaking, it's important to maintain a healthy mind-body connection. This is what helps you to focus and make the most of your energy.

When you are stressed out, tired and in a bad mood, you can't marshal your concentration to the point where you can really get the most out of your trading activity. For instance, if you are conducting research, you may not be able to focus enough attention on the charts and numbers you need to track. This may cause you to place trades in a haphazard fashion. Needless to say, this won't yield the best possible results.

Aside from the usual recommendations like eating healthy, getting exercise, and keeping stress at bay, it's worth noting that part of any successful trading plan involves taking care of your emotional wellbeing. On the whole, investing can get to be a bit stressful. While this doesn't mean that you will lose your hair from trading FOREX, the action can get a bit hot and heavy at times. For example, when you are under pressure after successive losses, you might feel compelled to make risky trades. Additionally, you may feel under intense pressure to make up your losses. While no one likes to lose, it's important to take losses in stride as much as you can. Losses are a part of life and should, therefore, be treated as such.

Another common issue with investors (this is very common among day traders) is that they tend to obsess with research. If you get caught up in the rigors of trading, you may end up becoming overly obsessed with conducting research and trading. As such, you might end up spending more time at your terminal than you should. This can lead to unhealthy habits, such as sitting down for too long. Also, it can take its toll on your mind, as trading is a very mental activity.

This is why successful investors look at FOREX as just another activity in their day. They set up routines and try to follow them as much as possible. They try to set a schedule that they know works for them. They also cap off their time at the terminal in order to avoid too much time in front of a screen. In doing this, they can refresh their mind and come back with more focus.

In particular, when you feel overwhelmed by too much data and information, taking time away can help you process the information that you have taken in. This is why playing sports, or engaging in any kind of physical activity, can help you clear your mind. When you do this, you are able to bounce back with more focus and energy. The last thing you want to do is put yourself in a position in which you are trudging along. If anything, trading FOREX is something which you should enjoy. Hence, forcing yourself to do it will never be conducive to obtaining successful results. So, do make an allowance for rest. Take care of your emotional and mental energy. You'll find that things get a lot easier that way.

CHAPTER 9

Most Popular Currencies In The Forex Market

By definition, trading FOREX is all about working with the world's entire currency supply. There are some currencies that are staples of the currency world, such as the US Dollar, the British Pound Sterling, the Japanese Yen, the Euro, and the Swiss Franc. Then, there are other important currencies such as the Canadian and Australian Dollar, Chinese Yuan, or the Mexican Peso.

All of these currencies are freely traded on the FOREX market, meaning that you can buy and sell them according to market prices and available supply. Consequently, you have every opportunity to make as much profit as you can based on your trades.

In the end, making a profit hinges on understanding the dynamics of the various currencies and the interactions. This largely depends on the relationships among countries and the frequency with which these currencies are traded together. Then, there are currencies that aren't usually traded together. In such cases, you need to be a bit more creative. Nevertheless, you can trade any currency at any time. It's up to you to do your homework on the best pairings that suit your particular investment strategy.

For example, if you choose to play it safe, then sticking to major currencies is your safest bet. If you are keen on making potentially significant gains, then you might try a road less traveled. This implies trading currencies which may not necessarily be commonly paired. It all boils down to the main objective you have in mind.

However, there is a word of caution here: for the novice investor, it's best to stick with more common currency pairings. As you gain more experience, you can venture out to other currencies. The important thing is to avoid taking on unnecessary risk at this point in the ballgame.

Major Currency Pairings

In the FOREX market, you'll find that certain currency pairs dominate the pace of the game. These pairs are called "correlated pairs" as they are commonly traded. Therefore, there is enough information to note that they move in accordance with the price action of each other. When one of the currencies has a significant shift, it directly impacts the other.

This is why understanding the nature of these pairings will enable you to make consistent profits. They may not be overwhelming, but they'll keep the lights on to be sure.

Here are the major currency pairs in the FOREX market today:

- The EUR/USD pair is the most commonly traded pair on the FOREX market. It accounts for roughly 20% of all transactions. For novice investors, this is the safest place to start. Here, you can find predictable results that will help you make money right from the start. You can copy-cat trades, too. That makes getting started even easier.

- The USD/JPY is generally regarded as the second-most traded pair. However, it does not account for nearly as much of the trading volume as the USD/EUR pair.

- The GBP/USD is also regarded as the third-place pair. This pair is generally traded on the European side of the market. Most American investors prefer the Euro.

- The USD/CHF pair is commonly traded as well though it does not account for nearly as much of the market share as some of the other pairs.

- Other interesting pairs include the USD/CAD, AUD/USD, and the NZD/USD. The NZD/AUD is also another correlated pair though its market share isn't nearly as significant as some of the other pairs on this list.

When you are first starting out in the FOREX market, it's best to stay with the major currency pairs. As we have mentioned earlier, you can get more creative as you gain more experience in the market. That is certainly valid as some unexpected pairings can provide you with the possibility of ample gains.

However, it's always best to do your research on these pairs before you take the plunge. While there is a good chance you'll clean up, there's also a good chance you'll fall short. So, do your homework before taking the plunge.

Determining the Price of Major Currency Pairs

The main reason why we recommend novice investors to deal with major currency is pairs is simple: volume. These are the currencies that attract the largest amount of transactions. As a result, novice investors can expect more bang for their buck, so to speak.

When there is a greater deal of trading volume, there is a greater chance for the strategies that we have highlighted throughout this book to work. When there is a smaller trading volume, the strategies which we have presented herein may not hold up quite as well. This is why dealing with lesser-known currencies should be done under very strict supervision.

That being said, the price of major currency pairs is set by supply and demand. This is why a large trading volume tends to minimize significant shifts in the price of major pairs. On the contrary, currencies that don't have a large trading volume may suffer significant shifts from a single trade. This can ultimately ruin your chances of making a profit.

With large, institutional investors, the kind that have positions in the millions of dollars, they tend to choose major currencies over lesser-known ones because the supply is large enough to hold such large trading positions. So, smaller investors can ride the coattails of large investors. When you trade along with the big firms, you can ride the top of the wave. This may not yield you millions of dollars, but it is certainly a great way of making a healthy profit.

For example, the EUR/USD rate sits at 1.10. This means that the cost of 1 Euro is $1.10. If the price suddenly moves to 1.12, it means that the Euro has gained value against the dollar as it costs more dollars to purchase a Euro. However, if the price drops to $1.08, then the dollar has gained value as it costs fewer dollars to purchase one Euro. Depending and what you're banking on, you can come out on top. The main thing to keep in mind is that the various factors in the market will ultimately determine the behavior of the price action among the major pairs. So, always be on the lookout.

Investing in Cryptocurrency

In recent years, cryptocurrencies, or cryptos, have become quite popular, especially after the meteoric rise of Bitcoin. The wild ride that saw Bitcoin soar to over $20,000 per coin landed cryptos on everyone's radar. Given the massive upside of cryptos, practically anyone that could get into the crypto market did. Unfortunately, some got hammered when the price of Bitcoin fell back down to Earth. Nevertheless, Bitcoin is not the only game in town.

Yet, cryptos are not widely understood by the average investor. That's why we are going to go over what cryptos are and how you can make money on from trading in cryptos. Additionally, you will find that cryptos are still in their infancy. This means that there is a massive upside which you can exploit.

It is important to underscore the fact that cryptos are not money in the traditional sense. A cryptocurrency is a type of digital token that can be used to settle transactions, among other uses. For instance, is one individual sells a car to another, the deal can be settled by exchanging digital tokens as opposed to using traditional currency. This is what makes cryptocurrencies so interesting to the average investor.

When you deal with cryptos, you are essentially dealing with 1s and 0s. These can be used for identification purposes, keeping track of volume, and even to facilitate government actions. Indeed, there are many types of uses for cryptos.

At this point, the expression of cryptos' value is seen in traditional currencies such as US Dollars. In this case, you can purchase cryptos by exchanging US Dollars (or any other accepted currency). The digital tokens are stored in a virtual wallet or vault. This vault contains the codes that lead to the access of your coins. You can then trade them to other users in exchange for other tokens, or traditional currency.

It should also be noted that cryptos don't trade like currencies do on the FOREX market. They trade more like commodities. A good example we can use to compare the value of cryptos is oil. Oil is a commodity and is traded at spot price. Spot price means the current price of the commodity at the time the trade is placed. Consequently, the same market forces apply here. Supply and demand are what drive the valuation of all cryptos. Some have an enormous issuance, such as millions of coins. Depending on their popularity, investors may choose to pay an increasingly higher value for them.

Trading Cryptocurrencies

Cryptos are not traded on the open market. This means that you need to go through a crypto exchange. These exchanges work in the same manner as FOREX does. The difference lies in that you are not trading "real" currencies. Rather, you are exclusively dealing with cryptos.

In a crypto exchange, you can use US Dollars, for instance, to purchase coins. You can then sell them back to other users for a profit or loss, depending on the outcome of the trade. Alternatively, you can choose to hold on to them as long as you wish. The main thing here is to be cognizant of the price.

Since price fluctuates freely, you need to pay attention to the quotes for standard cryptos. Thus, you can track their value and sell whenever you like. One thing to note here is that crypto trading is much simpler than FOREX. You don't need quite the complicated setup to trade cryptos. All you need is to buy and then sell. However, you need to keep your eye on the ball.

The good side of this is that cryptos don't have nearly the same trading volume as FOREX does. So, you shouldn't expect a second-by-second price action. You can determine the price action over much longer timeframes such as hours or even days. If you are proficient in chart reading, you can easily detect patterns in charts. Thus, you won't have to spend hours reading technical data.

Best Cryptos to Trade

This is a question that is commonly posed. For most folks, cryptos equal Bitcoin. As we have mentioned, Bitcoin is not the only game in town.

So, here are the top 10 cryptos you can trade today based on their market cap:

1. Bitcoin
2. Ethereum
3. XRP
4. Tether
5. Bitcoin Cash
6. Bitcoin SV
7. Litecoin
8. EOS
9. Binance Coin
10. Tezos

While this list is hardly exhaustive (there are over 5,000 cryptos in the market today), these offer the best chance for you to make some returns when trading. You can go on a crypto exchange like Coinbase to learn more about how you can open an account. Then, you can begin trading in these coins. The best thing about this list is that they all have varying prices. So, you don't have to shell out $10,000 for one Bitcoin. In fact, some trade for a little as a few pennies on the Dollar. As such, there is a price for everyone.

While there are other exchanges out there, the main thing to keep in mind is that the same rules apply. It's important to focus on reputable companies that offer a solid reputation and a good track record. Additionally, you will find that reputable crypto trade exchanges offer a great deal of support. After all, they are interested in facilitating trade as much as possible so that others can join. Consequently, you can expect to get a great deal of help when starting out trading cryptos.

CONCLUSION

Thank you very much for making it all the way to the end of this book. It has been quite a trip as we have covered a lot of information. We have gone over FOREX and how you can use this market to your full advantage.

So, the time has come for you to get started on the journey that is trading FOREX. At the outset of this book, we asked you not to begin trading until you made it all the way to the end. As such, we hope that you now feel confident in taking the plunge. While it might seem a bit daunting, don't worry. Every investor that starts out in this market often feels overwhelmed. The great thing is that you now have all of the tools you need to get started.

Please make the time to further your study of the FOREX market. It's imperative that you focus on improving your skills as much as possible. When you are committed to improving your skills, you will find that it's not nearly as hard as you might have thought. The only requirement here is to focus your concentration on making sense of the currency pairings you are studying. In this regard, going over charts, numbers, and technical data is essential in gaining the experience you need to become a great trader.

Also, please make sure that you follow the guidelines which we have outlined pertaining to choosing the right broker. In doing so, you will have made one of the most important decisions of your life. By choosing the right broker, you'll be able to give yourself the biggest advantage you could.

Now, please take the time to go over any parts of this book that you would like to dig deeper into. Do take the time to drill down as much as you can in any of the parts of this book. You will find that repetition is the best way to deepen learning. Moreover, you will always discover new things every time you read this book.

Furthermore, take full advantage of the free demo time reputable trading platforms provide. This time is highly useful in learning the ropes of FOREX trading without betting the farm. By the time you are ready to go live, you'll be confident in making the right types of deals. All you need is some time and practice to get up to speed.

So, thank you once again for taking the time to read this book. If you have found it to be useful, in any way, please tell your friends, family, colleagues, and associates about it. We are sure that they will also find it insightful. In particular, anyone who is looking to learn more about the exciting world of FOREX trading will surely find this book to be a great starting point.

The time has come to make some real money trading FOREX. What are you waiting for? Got get'em!